To Boy Scouts:
Change your life and the world

Dr. Carl A. True
Captain U.S. Navy (RET)

THOUGHTS OF DEEP THINKERS

"Whatever you do will seem insignificant, but it is most important that you do it. One must *be* the change one wishes to see in the world."

                       Mohandas Karamchand (Mahatma) Gandhi

"This is the true joy in life, the being used for a purpose recognized by yourself as a mighty one; the being thoroughly worn out before you are thrown on the scrap heap; the being a force of nature instead of a feverish selfish little clod of ailments and grievances complaining that the world will not devote itself to making you happy."

                       George Bernard Shaw

"Destiny is not a matter of chance, it is a matter of choice; it is not a thing to be waited for, it is a thing to be achieved."

                       William Jennings Bryant

Foreword

The search for good and ultimate truth is a time tested endeavor that has captured the imagination and energy of generation after generation of persons the world around. This search is seemingly inexhaustible and existential -- never ending and always taking one outside of themselves into the nether regions of the universe. We want to find GOOD, we want to be part of the good, and in the end we want to be consumed with the good rather than consumed with the search for the good.

What are we to do? **Enter Reverend Henri Rabb Ferger.**

For generations Henri found his truth in a way of life that taught, loved, modeled for, and mentored young boys and girls into their own discovery of good and truth. Henri's lesson began with a ring, a reading, and a square. It was simple in approach and introduction and was profound in its reach across lives, continents, and generations. Wherever life's journey took him, Henri lived it; he taught it to all who would listen, he gently reproved and encouraged his pupils, and he never lost faith that within each person lay this basic way of life in which one could find all the good they were ever searching for.

That is certainly the example we learn from Carl Nelson, who, when a young man searched for something, anything, good amidst the difficulties of boyhood. A chance week of his life, lived under the tutelage of Henri, and this way of good and truth were now open to him for a lifetime. This of course does not mean he always maintained vigor in his search, but it did mean this way of life was always present. He returned to the ring and square often and now counts it as the center of his search for good and truth.

The lesson, though found in the characteristics of a man, Jesus, whom many consider divine, is not overtly religious. It is though, overtly human. How do I order my life here on earth to be balanced? How do I get all I want out of life? How do I grow to be the best man or woman possible? Placed in the teachings of the Reverend Henri Rabb Ferger and illuminated by the story of Dr. Carl Nelson, the search for good and truth need not be an infinite existential exercise; rather it can be found today and lived all of your tomorrows.

Rev. Dr. Brian T. Parcel [ ]

DEDICATED TO AND IN HONOR OF

Reverend Henri Rabb Ferger

IN MEMORY OF

Hildur Nelson, Isabel Nelson Neubauer, Barbara Long Nelson

WITH THANKS TO

Dolores Hansen Nelson, Gordon Nelson, Martha Ferger, Gladys and Mitchell Howard, Carol Klepack, Kathryn Ferger, Margaret "Meg" Klepack, Drew Judd, Tedd Judd, Betty Judd, Pastor John and Toni Giffen, Pastor Brian T. Parcel, Pastor Hal and Shirley Kingsley, Bob Goodman, Peggy Lang, Jenni Busboom, the San Diego Writers/ Editors Guild, and especially the Division of Rare & Manuscript Collections in the Carl A. Kroch Library at Cornell University.

Read Carl Nelson's other books by placing your order at his website: www.carlanelson.us

Published Non-fiction Books

Import/Export: How to Take Your Business across Borders, 4rd Edition, McGraw-Hill, Inc., 2009.

International Business: A Manager's Guide to Strategy in the Age of Globalism, International Thomson Business Press, ITBP, 1999.

Exporting: A Manager's Guide to World Markets, ITBP, 1999.

Protocol for Profit: A Manager's Guide to Competing Worldwide, ITBP, 1998

Managing Globally: A Complete Guide to Competing Worldwide, Irwin, 1994.

Global Success: International Business Tactics for the 1990s, TAB-McGraw-Hill, 1989.

Your Own Import-Export Business: Winning the Trade Game, Global Business and Trade Communications, 1988

Published Novels

Madam President and the Admiral, New Century Press, 2008. Sequel to *Secret Players*. Nominated for Pulitzer.

Secret Players, New Century Press. 2003. Winner of the 2003 "best thriller" award by the prestigious San Diego Book Awards Association.

The Advisor (Cô-Vân), Turner, 1999. Won "best fiction" as judged by Southern California Writers Conference. Endorsed by Elmo R. Zumwalt, Jr., Admiral, U.S. Navy (Ret/Dec) and Robert S. Salzer, Vice Admiral, U.S. Navy (Ret/Dec).

Preface

The Message of the Puzzle Ring is simply about how to break loose from difficult circumstances and change your life. The book's premise is that change can be achieved by living a balanced life.

Reverend Henri Rabb "Pop" Ferger, who developed the message sometime between 1910 and 1912, presented it in the form of four major concepts: Mind, Body, Social Qualities, and Spirit (MBSQS), with a bit of self-motivation thrown in.

This book is meant to explain Pop's message and how it can be a foundation for you to become a four-square person and rise above your circumstance to do your chosen life's work.

With his Phi Beta Kappa and summa cum laude honors from Princeton, Henri could have been a professor of math and physics at any college in America. Instead, he went to India where he honed his simplistic message to guide young men. (In those times Indian women were not schooled.)

Henri proved to be a great teacher who spread his message along the dirt paths, jungles, and sidewalks of India, America, and many other countries – wherever his travels took him. During his journeys he offered his message to all people no matter their race, creed, or religion, those whose life was in limbo and wanted to rise but needed guidance to find their way. His hope was that by introducing the foundations of a balanced life, they would become strong self-motivated, contributing adults.

Some say Henri's message is obsolete – conceived too long ago -- out of date. Not so. The worldwide dropout rates and incarceration make it particularly relevant today. Life is about change, and Pop's message remains a significant model for finding balance in our unbalanced world.

Life is about change and Pop's simple message serves that need: "Strive to be a four-square person and chose a life's work that has meaning." Complimenting his message come two equally important reminders: the symbol of a square ☐ and a puzzle ring, both of which you will learn about in this book.

Every generation faces societal changes: morals, ethical standards, and life purposes. Many of today's young men and women still search for a mentor -- that special adult who will take the time to guide and uncover truths to their most demanding questions: What is a man or, for that matter, what is a woman? How do I become one? After whom should I pattern my life? Do I have the right to rise? How do I rise? What is my life's path?

This true story is about Henry's life work and his effect on a boy of twelve (the author) who met the older gentleman merely ten days in 1943 and only once again 40 years later. Yet Henry's message became indelibly imprinted in the young man's mind, greatly affecting his growth. The sole purpose for the author's story is to show you what Pop's message can achieve.

"Pop," "Chief," or "Vijaiji," as Henri was often addressed, influenced me as well as thousands of others. I hope his message will do the same for you.

What Readers Can Learn

- Explains Henri's MBSQS message and its origin;
- Aims at troubled young adults (drop-outs, incarcerated) and their parents and mentors;
- Provides anecdotal stories based on the author's life as they relate to the MBSQS message and its value;

- Shows how to help others have a future – even if they have to navigate life without a mentor.;
- Enlarges upon the meanings of Henri's message as they apply to daily living;
- Explains the major historical issues happening in India during Henri and Kitty's time;
- Shows Henri's life work in India;
- Describes missionary life in India;
- Shows how and why Henri founded the first Boy Scout troop in North India;
- Encourages young adults to seek the higher road of life for success and happiness;
- Passes on the most important attitudes, principles, and skills that young adults must acquire before they can gain mastery of their character;
- Teaches effective ways of communicating to young adults about life's work with examples and metaphors they can understand;
- Explains a simple message for a life, full and free; and
- Builds confidence in parents' ability to mentor – to help their children by explaining the meaning of the simple MBSQS message.

About the Author

Carl Nelson is uniquely qualified to write this book, principally because he was one of Pop's boys. His experience in the field of mentoring was gained while serving on the military faculties at Annapolis and West Point, in command of Navy ships, at the Navy's personnel bureau, and as president of the Boys Club in Chula Vista, California, where he helped young men rise in their chosen careers. Carl grew up in the small town of Overbrook, near Pittsburgh, Pennsylvania. He is a graduate of the United States Naval Academy at Annapolis with a bachelors degree in engineering, a masters degree in economics/systems analysis from the Navy Post Graduate School Monterey, and a doctorate in international business (finance and trade) from Alliant/USIU University. He is a member of the Author's Guild, PEN USA, and a life member and past president of the San Diego Writers/Editors Guild. Dr. Nelson is listed in *Who's Who in California, Who's Who in America, Who's Who in American Education,* and *Who's Who in the World.*

In his first career, covering a span of 33 years, Carl rose from enlisted recruit to highly decorated Navy captain. He commanded the guided missile cruiser U. S. S. Worden CG-18, the Frigate U. S. S. Cook FF-1083, and the ocean salvage/tug U. S. S. Cocopa ATF-101. He served four tours of duty in the Vietnam War, three of which were at sea and one on the ground as commanding officer of U. S. sailors and Marines, fighting guerrillas in the Rung Sat Special Zone of the delta region of South Vietnam.

In his second career of 29 years, Carl became a widely-published, best-selling author whose novel *The Advisor (Co-van)* (based on his four tours of duty in the Vietnam War) was recognized as the "Best Work of Fiction" at the Southern California Writers Conference. *Secret Players,* his second novel, was voted "Best Thriller" in 2003 by the San Diego Book Awards Association. His third novel, *Madam President and the Admiral,* published in 2008, was nominated for a Pulitzer.

Seven of his eight non-fiction books in his academic field of international business and trade have also been published, including best-selling *Import/Export: How to Take Your Business Across Borders*, 4th Edition, 2009 (sales of over 200,000 books).

Carl and his wife Dolores live in Chula Vista, California, where he served as president of the Boys Club, co-founded the Boys and Girls Club, and served as president of the local Optimist Club. He is a member of Lodge 626 of F & A Master Masons, a 32-degree Scottish Rite Mason, and a life member of Vietnam Veteran Chapter 472.

Contents

Foreword i
Preface v
About the Author ix

Chapter 1	The Puzzle Ring 1
Chapter 2	Not for Fame, nor Power, nor Wealth 7
Chapter 3	Letter with the Message 17
Chapter 4	Along Came Kitty 33
Chapter 5	Measuring Growth 41
Chapter 6	Growing Up 47
Chapter 7	Teaching Boys in India 59
Chapter 8	Brig Time on Bread and Water 67
Chapter 9	Founding the Indian Boy Scouts 89
Chapter 10	Turning Points 99
Chapter 11	Good Bye, India 115
Chapter 12	Vietnam, the War 123
Chapter 13	Finding Pop 145
Chapter 14	New Life's Work (New Horizons) 155
Chapter 15	Facing Painful Times 161
Chapter 16	India - My Boyhood Dream 169
Chapter 17	Yesterday's Wisdom for Today's World 175
Chapter 18	My Last Letter to Pop 179
Appendix A	Bibliography 187
Appendix B	The Boy Jesus at the Temple 189
Appendix C	Understanding India's Culture 191
Appendix D	India in Henri's Time 193
Appendix E	Birth of Twin Nations 197
Appendix F	J. Fred Ferger Obituary 203
Appendix G	Founding the Boy Scouts 205
Appendix H	Guide with Helps 207

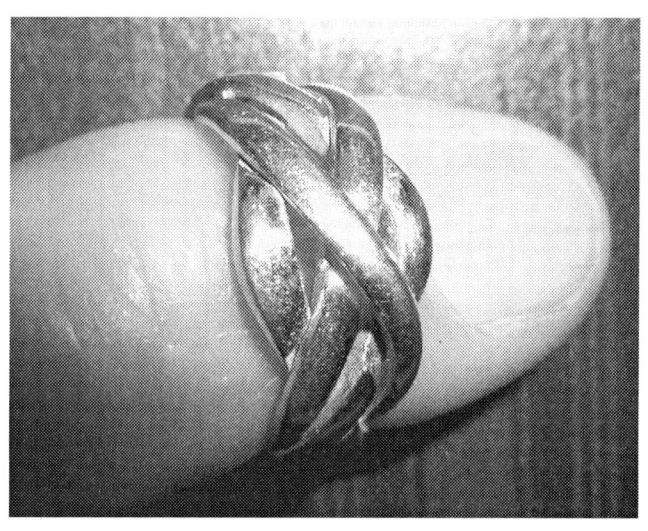

Chapter 1

The Puzzle Ring

It was a hot and humid July day in 1943 when my mother dragged me to a bus headed for a church camp in the mountains northeast of Pittsburgh, Pennsylvania. She made me dress as if I were bound for Sunday school at our local Presbyterian church instead of an outdoor camping experience. As we walked across freshly mowed grass and past tall deep-green trees, I tried to wrench my hand away from hers, but she wouldn't let go. I understand now why she acted the way she did. It was a very difficult time for her; she was determined to send me away from our circumstance: an alcoholic father who lived with another woman, and I was becoming her rebellious, out-of-control child.

On boarding the bus, I mumbled goodbye to Mom and joined a large group of strange kids, some of whom looked scared. I felt no fear even though it was my first time away from home. It turned out to be one of those uneventful trips where no one talked, not even me, but I wasn't a good talker, even then.

The cabins at Camp Greenwood were unpainted structures that smelled of raw lumber. I was assigned to loft #2 with seven other boys my age. As soon as we dropped our bags, we were introduced to our barracks counselor. Older and taller than my dad, the man had an imposing, square-jawed look of the generals we saw in the war movies every Saturday morning at the Melrose Theater. He got our attention with a soft-sounding, mossy, southern drawl, "Hello, boys. My name is Henri Ferger, but you can call me Pop. I'm on furlough from my post in India where I've worked as an educator and missionary for, so far, more than thirty years."

One boy, whose name I didn't know yet, asked, "How old are you, sir?"

I thought the boy was rude, but Pop didn't blink. He nodded at the boy and answered, "Why, I'm 54 years old." Then he turned to the rest of us, "Alright boys, how many of you know about India? Up, up, boys... raise your hands."

About half of us lifted our arms; some just wiggled their fingers.

"Good. Not bad," he said. "We'll try to improve on your appreciation of the land and its people before you go home."

For me India was as mysterious as the moon, but it quickly became a real place when Pop gave each of us a Hindu nickname. Mine was "Lamba Singh," the first word meaning tall.

Our daytime schedule included rigorous outdoor exercises like swimming, foot races, canoeing, and hiking. Although I was gangly and awkward, for me it was all fun -- playing sports and doing things I had never tried before.

In the coolness of the evening we began a routine of campfires, songs, and stories under a canopy of bright, sparkling stars. Sitting around a peaceful campfire we sang,

The Message of the Puzzle Ring

John Jacob Jingleheimer Schmidt, his name is my name too, whenever I go out, the people always shout, "There goes John Jacob Jingleheimer Schmidt." Dah, dah, dah, dah, dah, dah, dah. We repeated the verse over and over, each time singing more softly until it was lip-synced, and finally we sang the last verse very, very loud.

Not long after our camp program began, Pop gathered us near the bottom steps leading to our second floor bunkroom. He told us a little bit about India and that he was a high school principal there. He added, "My students are Hindu, Muslim, and Buddhist boys… " He scratched his head and added, "Come to think of it, there might have been a few Jewish boys too. Well … I teach them in English and sometimes in their own languages; Hindi and Urdu. We also have several Boy Scout troops."

I thought it interesting that he spoke three languages. I was having a hard time in just one.

Pop held up an Indian puzzle ring (see photo), the kind made up of four lesser rings woven in such a way that they could be worn together on a finger.

Speaking in a quiet tone that I surmised was a mixture of southern American, British English, and Hindu, he said, "Now, boys, I have a challenge for you." He shook the ring apart, demonstrated several times how to put it back together, then slipping the ring on his finger, added, "You'll note that singly the four lesser rings of the puzzle are just an unbalanced mess. When put together correctly they make a whole, wearable ring, just like your lives can be a mess if you are not a four-square person. Thus when the ring is together it represents four simple words: "MIND - BODY - SOCIAL QUALITIES – SPIRIT (MBSQS), and these can be a foundation for anyone to *rise* (he emphasized this word) above their circumstances and do important things.

"You can think of the lesser rings as representing each of those four words and the wearable ring representing the well-rounded or four-square person."

He took off the ring, shook it apart, and asked, "All right, who wants to take the challenge? Who wants to be first? If you succeed, you may keep the ring."

Standing on the landing above, I watched carefully each of Pop's demonstrations and the boys as they struggled to win the prize. Truthfully, I was more interested in the ring than the four words I didn't even understand. But I *did* want to become a man, whatever that was. The challenge of the ring caused a rush of adrenalin. My stomach felt nervous, just as it did before any competitive activity.

Finally, after all the other boys had failed, Pop looked up at me and said gently, "Lamba Singh, you're the only one who hasn't tried. You need not if you don't want to, but you won't know what you can do in life until you try."

I knew the trick, yet I felt too shy to volunteer. I had watched carefully as Pop held two of the lesser rings together, then rotated the other two in place to form the wearable ring.

But what if I fail?

The other boys were already taunting me because I was so skinny and clumsy. I couldn't run or swim as fast as they. Failure at one more thing would only increase my pain. On the other hand, if I could do just one thing better than they, I might be accepted.

My body tensed. My stomach churned. My voice cracked as much from lack of confidence as from my changing body. I said, "I... I, I'll try."

With shaking hands, I took the jumbled mess of four lesser rings and began to replicate what I believed was the secret.

"Oh, Lamba Singh won't be able to do it," one of the boys said with a giggle.

Pop cautioned, "Give him his chance, boys. Be fair. You had your turns."

I was halfway through my attempt when I realized I was not doing it exactly right. I shook the rings to begin again.

"He's had his chance. He can't do it," another boy exclaimed.

Pop held up his hand and said, "Let him go. I think he's on to it."

All at once I felt calm. Everything went silent except for a bird singing in a nearby tree. At that moment I knew I could do it, and without further hesitation I proceeded to solve the puzzle.

I handed the ring in its wearable form to Pop.

Like a father, he put his hand on my shoulder and said, "No, it's yours. Put it on your finger and hand me your Bible." He drew a small square ☐ at the end of St. Luke 2:52 and next to it wrote, "Pop Ferger, 25 July '43." Across the top of the page he wrote, MIND - BODY - SOCIAL QUALITIES - SPIRIT.

Then he said to us boys, "I caution all of you that it's the words, not the art of putting the ring together, that's important. Remember the story of Jesus in Luke 2:52. It tells us that Jesus was becoming a well-rounded person, not a single-faceted one. To be like Him, that is Jesus-like, is to follow that scripture.

"And Jesus increased in wisdom and stature, and in favour with God and man."

How did I feel? My chest swelled – I thought I would explode and burst through the top of the world! I had done something no one else could do.

Through the daze of what I had done I heard one of the boys say, "So?" There was a taint of jealousy to his tone.

"So what?" Pop asked.

"So, what if we become well rounded."

"Then you'll rise and become a good man."

Another boy asked, "Then what, sir?"

"Why, then as a man you may be in a position to do good for others – universal humanity."

After that I remember that the boys of loft #2 treated me much better after that.

On my return to Pittsburgh, I raced straight to my waiting mother. In the middle of asking me if I had a good time, I interrupted and began relating the many games we played. I finally showed her the ring.

She smiled and examined my precious achievement. Pop Ferger, who returned on the bus with us, was standing nearby. He introduced himself and told her the rest of the story. Before returning to his wife in New Jersey and eventually to his life's work in India, he stayed at our home and visited our church over the weekend.

The only thing I knew about Pop was his name and the puzzle ring message. As he was leaving, I asked him, "Will I ever see you again?"

"Maybe not. But we can correspond. Will you write to me in India?'

"Sure."

He reached out and shook my hand, like a man.

"Shall we be pals for life?" he asked.

"Sure," I responded

His departure left me with unanswered questions: What is a man? Can I live up to Pop's message – a way of life with wisdom -- a four-square person? I also wanted to know more about the country called India.

I felt very sad, but real men weren't supposed to cry, and I wanted to be one. So I didn't, although tears welled up just under the surface. This was a man I could trust, and I would never forget him. Pop would live on in my memory the rest of my life as my secret friend, and though I would not meet him again for 40 years, his message stuck with me, all that time, like super glue, like a bug on fly-paper, and it ultimately changed my life.

Henri Ferger

Chapter 2

Not for Fame, nor Power, nor Wealth

I suppose my connection to Pop Ferger could seem to others like an unusual obsession for a twelve-year old. I didn't agree with that then and still don't. For me there's nothing wrong with admiring an elder. Who knows what influence can bring to boys and girls as a result of a friendship with an adult. It's called mentoring – like a teacher, an advisor, or a trainer. Too many adults don't realize their influence as mentors to the young.

I now think of Pop as a heroic man because he didn't talk about his message for fame, or power, or wealth; he just did it as a human spirit -- for service to humanity – so that others would become better persons.

His letters, postmarked from various places in India, continued to arrive. Each letter always came with the words "Mind, Body, Social Qualities, and Spirit" across the top, a square penned next to the salutation, and with his nickname "Pop" at the end. After skimming the letters, I carefully filed them to read again, someday.

He was 54 years old and I was 12 when I met him in 1943, and he had already been at his life's work as a missionary teacher and school principal in India for 33 years. I knew nothing of this then, but the more I learned about Pop, the more I admired him and wanted to know more.

I even imagined a visit with him in India and told myself, "I want to do that some day."

Thinking about what I might do for my own life's work, I began to wonder how Pop decided to become a missionary and why. Definitions of "life's work" vary among the many books I've read. Some people are quite happy to have a job, period. Their goal is to work for one company for a lifetime. There's nothing wrong with that, although it is not today's reality – most jump from company to company before they settle. Others believe that during their 70 or 80 years on earth, their lives should make some contribution to humankind.

Have you thought about your life's work? You are one of approximately seven billion people on planet Earth, and there is a lot to be done. What will your contribution be? Will you be interested in science, sociology, or being a builder, physician, or missionary? Don't be afraid to think about your future. One of the things I've learned about Pop's puzzle ring message is that your life is at stake. It's OK to say to yourself, "When I'm 55 or 60 years old, what do I want my life to be like?" You may not rise to your goal in one big step, like graduation from medical school or qualification as a welder. Maybe you'll start and stop a few times, but sooner or later most chose something that has meaning for them.

I thought of Pop's work in that manner. He was helping young people rise to make a contribution while living a free, full life modeled after Jesus. But his letters indicated his decision to go to India didn't come instantaneously.

It wasn't until mid-2000 that I began to gather what I would write about Pop's life. I still had most of his letters stored away in good order, but I lacked much information about his life in India. Off I went on a research safari. This book comes from personal interviews and those letters exchanged between me and Pop over a 40-year period. Other information was gathered from interviews with the Ferger family and from Henri's papers in the Division of Rare & Manuscript Collections, Carl A. Kroch Library, Cornell University.

Henri was born on July 10, 1889, and he grew up in America's deep South. To this day I don't know why his first name ends in "i." A family member thought the spelling came from a French ancestor on his mother's side. I also wondered how a man from a southern region of America decided to become an educator and missionary in such a far-off place as Rawalpindi, India.

Chattanooga, where Pop grew up, was a city torn apart in 1863 by General Grant's ruthless charge during the Civil War. The city is situated in the southeast corner of Tennessee on the eastern side of the Appalachian Mountains near Lakes Chickamauga and Nickajack, both of which flow into the Tennessee River. Major battles were fought there including Lookout Mountain, but after the war, the people undertook extensive reconstruction. Today Chattanooga is the fourth-largest city in Tennessee and no longer looks like those towns described in *Gone With the Wind*.

From 1905-1907 Pop attended Chattanooga University. At the end of his second year, he transferred to Princeton

University and, after marching in the 1907 freshman parade, began the course of instruction in science.

At Princeton Henri was the kind of student who lived the four-square ☐ life. He studied hard, went to chapel every day, and participated in a full range of extra-curricular activities. When, on June 10, a month before his 21st birthday, he was notified that he had made the Phi Beta Kappa society, he humbly said, "I'm very surprised -- God's hand."

Henri reacted the same way when he learned that he ranked third among all the students in the Princeton science department. At graduation he received the degree of Bachelor of Science, cum laude, with honors in math and physics.

One reason Henri might have chosen missionary work was that in his senior year at Princeton, the president of Union College of New York gave an inspirational sermon to a large crowd – the topic: "Life's Work." Apparently that talk had such a significant effect on Henri that shortly thereafter he volunteered to do several weeks as a "Big Brother" at the New Jersey State Home for Boys (a reformatory). These were problem boys with few or no expectations. Their parents were low-income, blue-collar with little background to encourage growth. Sentenced to strengthen their character, the delinquents often chose fighting and joined gangs. With little else to do, they hung out and found trouble. They could see only one thing: bodies for street toughness -- and seldom knew anything about how to use their minds or social qualities or spirit. Henri soon found that he got along well with his charges -- they liked him as much as he liked them, probably because he was such a good teacher.

Henri went on to spend two summers at a YMCA camp. During this period Henri probably began thinking about a simple message to help boys improve their lives and motivate them to rise. He wanted it to be like the attention span of boys -- short and snappy. He came up with the four simple words: "Mind, Body, Social Qualities, and Spirit," and envisioned the message, patterned after Jesus in Luke 2:52, to be like scattering seeds – just spread the idea of the four-square person. He gave many seminars about these four foundation words in the hope that somehow the seeds would just take root, grow, and help youth become better persons seeking a full and free life in an increasingly complex and changing world.

Pop had a long discussion with his father about the concept of "life's work." J. Fred "Pappa" Ferger was a prominent citizen of Chattanooga. Pappa discouraged Henri from missionary work, suggesting, "Return home with me and join the family business."

Assured there would be an opening in the New Jersey Boys Reformatory on his return from India, Henri signed a contract, on August 29, 1910, to become a missionary for the Student Volunteer Movement. That organization sent him to the Christian Mission in the Punjab, then a state in Northwest India, to teach for three years.

Henri spent his last full day before leaving for the Punjab visiting with his family at their home at 830 Vine St, Chattanooga. During an auto ride with Pappa, they again talked about life's work. Pappa asked, "What might you do in the event the mission assignment is not to your satisfaction?" Henri responded, "Pappa, I'll teach in India for two to three years and then make up my mind."

Off he went to Gordon Mission College in the city of Rawalpindi to teach science and math.

Why Rawalpindi?

Maybe he saw the romance of living in one of the most historically important places on earth. Also known as Pindi, the city is located near Islamabad, now the modern capital of Pakistan, in the Indian province of Punjab near the Margalla Pass. This place served as the crossroads of the earliest habitations of man in Asia.

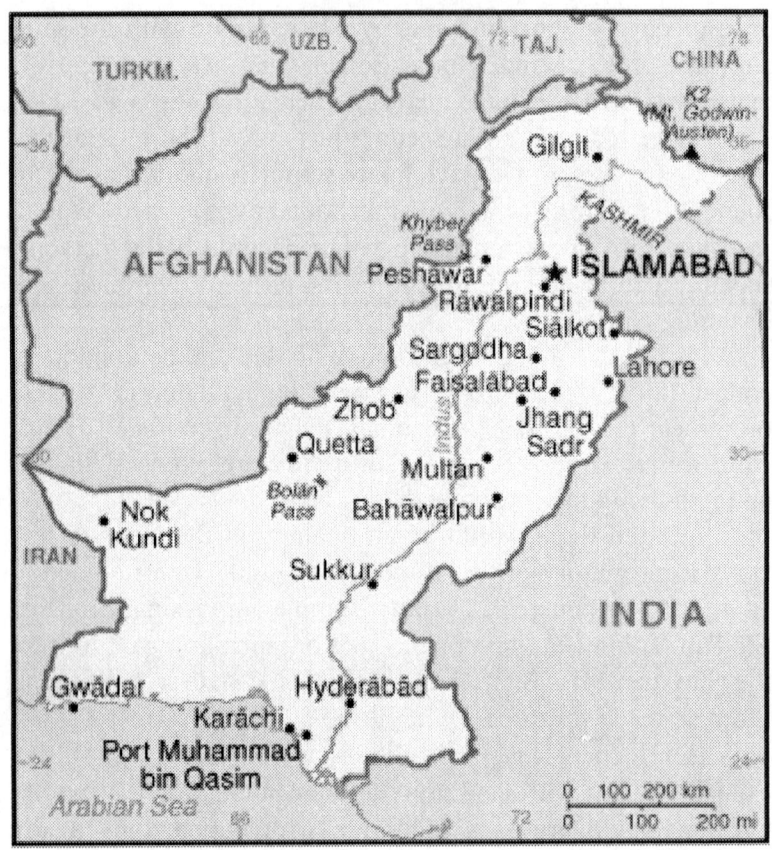
Source: Wikipedia, 2007; (the pale area is present day Pakistan)

At one end of the ancient Indus Valley the earliest stone implements were made on a mass scale and sent down to the lower reaches of the Indus River. As the first settlement of Aryans from Central Asia, it was also on the route through which passed all those who invaded India from the north and northwest. The large number of languages still spoken there is evidence of the many ethic groups that have passed through. The people of that region witnessed ancient caravans as well as the bloody onslaught of the ferocious armies of Alexander, Genghis Khan, and Tamurlane. The banks of the River Soan in Rawalpindi hosted Stone-age man over 7000 years before modern India and Pakistan. Human skulls dating back to 5000 B.C. have been found in and around that area.

Henri was a meticulous man who kept a diary with precise notes on everything, which permitted him to write excellent, newsy letters. As an example of his attention to detail he wrote, "Left home in Chattanooga at precisely 5:39 p.m., August 30, 1910, and sailed from New York at exactly 10 p.m., September 6th, 1910, aboard Kaiser Wilhelm II of the North German line. He went on to say, "Good weather -- clear and very warm."

Traveling by way of Plymouth, Cherbourg, and Paris, he saw first hand that although World War I had not yet started, Europe was already near boiling.

Changing ships in Marseilles, he sailed to Macedonia then on to Port Said. Following the transit of the Suez Canal, he arrived, according to his precise notes, "September 30th, at Bombay and at 5:49 at Rawalpindi just 32 days, lacking 10 minutes after leaving home."

At Gordon Mission College, Henri met a Mr. Scott, who told him, "You'll do two classes in biology and one in math."

Thus, in the fall of 1910, the six-foot tall, bone-skinny, imposing Caucasian with brown hair, blue eyes, and a mustache, began his life's work.

Pause now to visualize Henri on his first day standing on the bare floor of an unpainted classroom with only wooden benches and a chalkboard. He would certainly have been uneasy teaching dark-skinned Hindu and Muslim boys using American English. Food, that might have included the most popular dishes to Hindus, like "Masala Dosa" and "Rasgolla," could take some time to get used to. He might have been surprised to learn there were three castes, at least three religions, many languages, and many cultures. But the lack of educational opportunities available for girls would have startled him. "Where are the girl students?" He might have asked again, "Are there no schools for women?"

His son, Dr. John Ferger, commented, "In those days, he was painfully shy, rather inarticulate, and ill at ease with young people. That he overcame these traits is a tribute to his dedication to his work as a missionary."

His students, all boys, seemed to like him, even though he was a strict disciplinarian. They would have been flipping pages of their bi-lingual dictionaries in their scramble to keep up. When class was over he would have dismissed the boys with, "Tomorrow, besides your science lesson, we will talk about Jesus as a boy. Read St. Luke 2:52 in the Christian Bible."

Before he would leave for the evening, several of the students would rush forward with questions about the lesson. A bold one, who spoke excellent British English would ask, "What does Jesus have to do with biology?" Another might have said, "But I'm a Muslim. Do I have to read the Bible?"

The American would smile serenely and, like a father, gently touch the boy's shoulder and patiently answer, "I'll let you know tomorrow."

Returning to his small room that smelled of herbs, spices, and incense, he would eat a bit, pray a bit, and agonize about staying in India. In loneliness he would permit his mind to flash back to his hometown in Tennessee where he had grown up in an upper-middle-class neighborhood. His reminiscence might have focused on Princeton University where the brick buildings are constructed for the ages, not like the rickety ones in Rawalpindi where he taught boys in a language foreign to them. Not an easy job even in New York City.

Depressed at the challenge before him, we know he took pen to paper and wrote a letter home to his mother and father, "At present, I do not feel as if I want to make this my life's work."

The next day he brought his math and science students his Christian Bible and his roughly developed message about a four-square life (MBSQS). He emphasized to the boys that,

"Just because it is based on the a verse from the Bible in St. Luke 2:52, it can be useful to help you rise no matter who you worship, the God of Hindus, Muslims, Christians, Jews, or Buddhists, or none at all. Christ is a way, but there may be other ways as well. Seek the right path for you to be Christ-like -- that will help you have a free, full life."

Later that first year he asked those same boys, "Have you heard of the new game called volleyball?"

"No, sir," they responded in unison.

One of the students asked in his heavy Indian accent, "What is it, sir?"

"Well, it's a new game recently invented in America ... well 15 years ago, back in 1895 by a man named William Morgan at a YMCA in Holyoke, Massachusetts. It's a game played with an inflated ball passed back and forth across a high net. Would you like to learn it?"

"Yes," came the resounding answer from boys who would rather play than study.

So it was that Henri Ferger not only introduced his MBSQS message but a new game to India. He ordered a ball, net, and rules, and that became the beginning, for India, of what is now a universally-played game and a part of the Olympics.

Later on that first year he told a few of his teacher friends that he was ambivalent about staying. One, who knew of his success with his boys, told him, "Maybe you should go back and become a minister, then return."

Pop had taken his Princeton degree with the intention to become an educator, but on May 31, 1911, less than a year after he began teaching, he wrote home, "It's been about one year since acceptance. Never have I been sorry of it at all."

What changed his mind? Was it the challenge of teaching Hindu and Muslim boys or his teacher friend's suggestion that he become ordained? Another reason to change his mind might have been that he came from a close, well-educated family, one that looked not for a job but rather sought a "life's work." He could have realized that MBSQS was for him as well as for his boys and applied it to his own growth. Whatever caused the change, whether at the time he recognized it or not, he would become a devotee of educating and ministering to boys as they grew to manhood.

At the end of his three-year contract, Henri took his friend's advice and made arrangements to return to America to begin studies with the intent to earn a Ph.D. at the same time he would study to become ordained.

On arriving in New York on September 22, 1913, he noted, "Engaged a room at an apartment on West 122 Street. $3.00 per week."

To supplement his income, he showed slides and gave talks about India while wearing costumes and turbans or *Pagri*. He earned $5.00 each from as many as 100 boys who also learned his message about the puzzle ring.

By early April of 1915, he dropped the idea of staying on to earn a doctorate. Instead he simultaneously completed a masters degree at the Teachers College of Columbia University and his work at the Union Theological Seminary. About that same time he curiously began spending more time at the New Jersey State Home for Boys.

It was then that his diary made first mention of the name Kitty. It simply said, "Kitty's birthday."

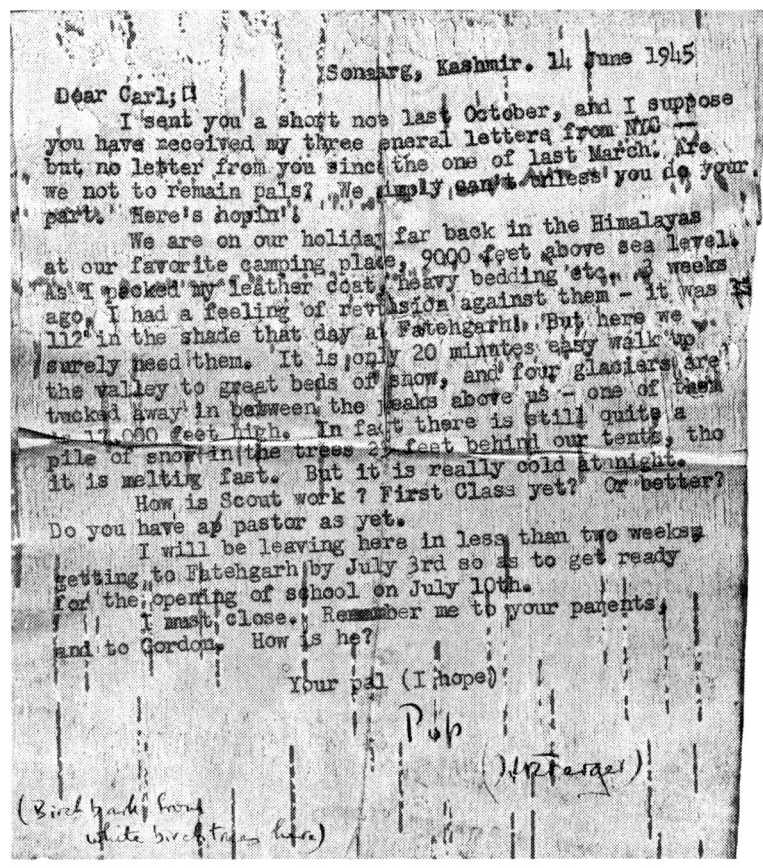

Pop's letter from Kashmir, India, written on birch bark

Chapter 3

Letter with the Message

I found family life in India very fascinating, but of course I knew nothing about that until 1943 when I won the puzzle ring and learned the kind of life Henri thought we should pursue. I'm certain there are some boys and girls that have lived a perfect four-square life, but I can only tell you about my life, which has had ups and downs. When I say ups and downs I really mean it. I have not been perfect, as you will soon find out.

You might wonder how Pop, a missionary living so far away as India, could become the inspirational figure of my life based on a one-week period at Camp Greenwood. You might even have doubts that I, a 12-year old boy at the time, could be that affected, but I was and still am.

I'm not sure why we took to each other. For him it might have been the satisfaction of seeing boys better themselves. As for me, maybe I thought about his mentoring wisdom because I lacked a male image – my own dad was often drunk. Or maybe it was my thoughts about foreign places and the mysteries of India where I swore secretly to go some day, or it might have been my success with the puzzle ring, or, more likely, I was just a dreamy eyed kid.

In those days I often lay awake wondering about Pop, India, and his message. The puzzle ring I'd won became a metaphor not only for a well-rounded, four-square life, but also for the concept of rising to manhood and experiencing a free and full life modeled after Jesus. That, I'm sure, was exactly what Pop wanted us boys to remember.

When I turned thirteen in the fall of 1943, a chilled Pittsburgh wind filled the air blowing brown and red leaves all over our yard. It was the day the mailman brought a letter from Pop postmarked New Jersey. I knew he was spending the remainder of his furlough with his wife Kathryn and son John, then a student at Swarthmore College, who would remain behind to continue his studies when Pop returned to India. His letter explained, "Our two-and-a half years in America will end next spring. We will be returning to India by boat and be back on the job by August of 1944. In the meantime I'll continue to give my lectures about the four-square life. I call them, 'We Visit the World' and 'The Meaning of the Ring.'"

I told my mother about Pop's letter and their return trip to India. She set the hot iron on its flat end then took a long drag on her Lucky Strike. Looking at me through sad eyes, she said, "That'll be a very dangerous voyage, son. Nazi submarines are sinking our ships every day as they cross the Atlantic. Henri and his wife could be killed."

Her words caused chills to vibrate up and down my adolescent spine. Until then, World War II, the war that America and its allies were fighting against Germany, Italy, and Japan all over the world, was just a game I played with my friends in the basement of our house.

I was in the seventh grade when Pop and Kitty sailed east from Philadelphia in March of 1944. Their trip, as my mother prophesized, would be in very dangerous waters. As a security measure, Henri and his wife were not allowed to know even the date of their departure until just before sailing.

For the first time, for me, World War II became a reality: A person I actually knew and cared about, my secret pal, was in danger.

*****

I'd like to tell you that my rebellious, stupid stage stopped immediately after I won the puzzle ring, but it didn't.

It got worse.

Maybe a similar thing has happened in your life.

My dad often came home drunk. He spent his pay buying drinks for his pals at the local Overbrook tavern. After he and mom separated, she seemed to be mad all the time, screaming and shouting, especially at me.

I still believe the reason I lost my dad to alcohol was because of World War II, though he never served.

This story really begins in Pittsburgh on a Saturday morning in the spring of 1943, the same year I met Pop

Ferger. Some weeks before, when my dad started drinking again, my mother kicked him out of the house. She told me he had a girlfriend. After that she shouted at me constantly – I seemed always to be under her feet, doing everything wrong.

When dad returned that morning, his breath smelled of alcohol and his words slurred from a voice that sounded like he was drunk. At the front door he pleaded forgiveness. His eyes shed a few tears. My mother slammed the door in his face and locked it. He then tried to muscle his way back in by racing around the house to the back door. Mom and I took the short cut through the dining room and got there first in time to lock the screen door and tell him to leave. He threatened to break the door. When he put his fist through the screen, that's when I ran for my gun.

In my bedroom, I found my rifle, loaded it with BB's, and returned to stand beside my mother. Pointing it at the drunken man I loved, I said, "Leave her alone."

She shouted at me, "Put that gun away – are you stupid? He's your father."

Mom struggled with him and pushed his hand away and locked the door.

Dad went away and never came back.

I didn't cry, but I wanted to. I would miss him.

World War II, for the people of the United States, began on December 7, 1941. I had just turned eleven years old the previous October. Some of you might remember the most famous day in our history, the Sunday when airplanes of the Japanese Navy bombed the American fleet moored to the docks or anchored in the harbor at Honolulu, Hawaii. Before that day our country had been battling back from a great economic depression that caused about 25 percent of Americans to be unemployed. That attack infuriated every one of our 132 million people and gave President Franklin Delano Roosevelt a good reason to call upon the population of our entire nation to pitch in and fight every way we could.

That included my dad, Alfred Helge Axel Nelson, a first generation Swedish-American (In those days he was just called Swede) who was exempt from being drafted as a soldier because he had an epileptic health problem and was the father of two boys. But Dad did his part by continuing to work at a Standard Oil petroleum plant located in Pittsburgh on the Allegheny River.

The war effort immediately transitioned America from a mediocre nation to the world's super power and provided my little brother Gordon, who was seven, and me a window on the world war by way of radio and newspapers.

Our mother Isabel, who kept a tight rein on her two high-energy boys, made sure we were aware of what was happening in the world. Names like Nazi, Japs, and Allies were constantly bandied about. We often played war in the basement of our house at 2038 Dartmore and the heavily-treed woods across the street.

Dad had to work long hours, but according to him, it was for a good cause and good money. In fact, I remember him saying that his annual salary doubled from about $2,000 a year to $4,000 in the first two years of the war. Our folks took us on vacations during the summers and to baseball games at Forbes field. For us life seemed as good as it gets. Pittsburgh was not exactly the apple pie of our nation but more like a mixture of middle-income, blue collar Catholic immigrants from Eastern Europe, and a sprinkling of white Anglo-Saxon Protestants (WASPs). Yet we all got along very well.

The war brought the good times with jobs and big money, but with it came the darkness of grief for dead soldiers. Booze washed it all away. With their new-found money, our parents took to card parties and heavy drinking which led to arguments over who won the poker hand and laughter from the latest dirty jokes. The evenings ended with them staggering away from the dining room table and making their way home.

If Saturday was party night, Friday was payday. My dad, like many blue collar workers, received his pay in cash at the end of the week. It became a habit that men stopped on the way home for a 'puddler and helper' (whiskey and beer) at the local Overbrook bar. My dad could make it to the bar but had difficulty continuing home. On those occasions when he was late, my mother would tell me, "Go... Get your dad and bring him home. If he won't come, bring what's left of his pay."

On two or three occasions I walked that mile, nervous at first, but by peeking in the window, I could see he was sitting at a corner stool. A woman sat nearby. One of his friends pointed at the window and Dad came out, brought me in, and introduced me to his pals. That time he drove me home, no trouble. After that he wasn't so cooperative – although he did give me his payday money to take home to mom. His habits began to change -- some days he didn't come home at all. Mom would scream and cry when he finally came in. They would make up and he would stop drinking for a few weeks. After a while the drinking would start again, and she would kick him out of the house again, and finally she wouldn't let him back.

That was the Saturday morning my mother became a single mom long before that became ordinary, and I lost my father to alcohol.

As I grew and my moody feelings worsened, I became a loner whose grades fell like a stone hitting the bottom of a deep pit. I dropped out of church and Boy Scouts, quit writing to Pop, joined a gang, skipped church, began smoking cigarettes, and got caught stealing from a drug store. I drank my first beer in the back seat of George Frazier's junk-heap car, and the Overbrook police picked me up for throwing stones at billboard lights.

One of my stupid acts was starting fights, for no reason, with my friend George Frazier. I don't know who started it, we were not bullies, but we would go to war on the way home from school. When our mothers learned of it, the law struck like a woodchopper's hammer. Immediately my mother organized a boxing match with big gloves in our front yard. She would be the referee, and when the match was over, we would shake hands and never fight each other again.

Looking back, I admire George for boxing me in my yard, but it was what the mothers had agreed to. George was shorter than me but wiry and quick. We put our hands up, gloves twirling, moving in slow circles and waited nervously until my mother called out, "begin."

George fought from a crouch; I, on the other hand, began with my left hand jab. Round and round we postured, never touching the other until my mother shouted, "Hit, hit each other. You like to fight so much, now is your chance." George through a left hook and we were into it. Each hit the other, mostly on the arms, occasionally on the face. It was not long before we were sweating and breathing hard. Mother made us box one more round. By then we were exhausted. She asked, "Had enough?"

When neither of us answered she asked, "Oh, you want more?"

"No mam," we said in unison.

"OK, shake hands and say after me, "I promise not to fight each other ever again."

"I promise…"

And so it was over.

****

Even though my fighting was over, I still felt angry about everything and nothing. With only a gym bag holding one suit of underwear, an extra pair of socks, and a toothbrush, I took to the roads heading west. I had no idea where I was going, but in those days truckers and cars often picked up hitchhikers. I made it all the way to Columbus,

Ohio, but I remember how sad I felt when I was standing alone on an empty road to nowhere. Tears came to the surface but I wouldn't let them overflow; real men don't cry. Right then I thought of the puzzle ring message, and it sparked in me the realization that I was going in the wrong direction. I reversed course and fled back toward Pittsburgh. On the return trip, a truck driver reached across the cab to touch the inside of my leg. I was very naive and at first had no idea what he was doing. When his rub brought on an erection, I immediately swatted his hand away and sat up tall and silent with frozen fists ready to fight. At the next stop I jumped out of his truck.

Returning home at the break of daylight, I climbed a ladder to my mother's bedroom. She must have heard me as I crawled in the window, because she sat up and, with both hands, silently motioned me to come to her. She didn't say anything, just wrapped her arms about me, drew me to her chest, and let me fall asleep.

While I was away on my hitchhiking escape, a letter shown at the beginning of this chapter came from Pop. It was mailed from Sonaarg, Kashmir, India, on June 14, 1945, two years after I'd met Pop. It was written on white birch bark with the symbol of the square ☐ while he and his wife were on vacation at 9000 feet in the Himalaya Mountains. In it he chided me for not keeping up my correspondence.

As I read it, I noted that the dates on the first letter fell approximately halfway between V-E (Victory in Europe) day (May 8) and V-J (Victory in Japan) day (August 15). I vividly remember both those dates because when the radio blared the announcements, everyone in America ran into the streets shouting, setting off fireworks, and screaming, "The war's over, the war's over!"

In a second letter, Pop painted a picture of a world at war with bombs raining on cities in Europe and the Pacific Islands. Yet, giving God credit, he and his wife Kitty crossed the Atlantic safely. Sailing at best speed in a darkened, zigzagging ship they had arrived in Lisbon, Portugal, in April 1944. Because of the dangers, they had to remain there until after the D-Day landings in June. In this letter he included information that their son John (born January 12, 1924, six years before me) had remained behind in America. Having grown up in India and finished high school at the world-famous Woodstock School in Mussoorie, he had gone to the United States in 1940 to enter Swarthmore College intending to eventually become a physician.

Finding another vessel bound for India, Pop and his wife sailed across the Mediterranean to East Africa and on to Bombay. They arrived in August at a place called Fatehgarh, a twin city to Farrukhabad, in the state of Uttar Pradesh in Northern India. This place they would call home was on the right bank of the Ganges River.

The foreign names he used in his letters sounded interesting and romantic. How I yearned to visit those places some day!

Until I read Pop's letters, I didn't know with certainty that he and his wife, Kathryn, whom I hadn't met, had arrived safely in India. Now I was elated. While others were shouting, "The war's over," I was shouting, with tears forming just below the surface, "He's alive! He's alive."

After reading his letter, I felt ashamed -- I was guilty of not doing my share of letter writing. I immediately took pen to paper.

Dear Pop ☐
I'm all right. Thanks for your letters. I'll try to do better with my own. Went swimming yesterday. Going to visit my aunt tomorrow. I'm starting high school this year. It starts soon.
Sincerely,
Lamba Singh ☐

In less than a month I received his response. Pop's letters were always longer than mine. This one included the following form letter that I think he sent to all his boys.

"*Dear Lamba Singh:* ☐

I hope you still wear your well-earned puzzle ring and remember to associate it with the last verse of the second chapter of the Gospel of St. Luke: "And Jesus increased in wisdom and in stature and in favor with God and man."

You will recollect that this verse comes just after the account of the journey of Jesus at the age of twelve (the same age you were when we met at Camp Greenwood) with his parents for the first time to the holy city of Jerusalem and the great Passover Festival.

One who has seen the East can better understand the many new interesting sights that the boy Jesus saw in the Temple and bazaars of that great city. On the first night of the return journey Jesus did not join his parents at the time of the evening meal.

If a boy does not turn up at suppertime, his parents know that something is wrong. So after searching through the caravan, they returned the same night to Jerusalem, and on the third day found him in the Temple.

The enclosed painting shows Jesus explaining to his parents why he stayed behind at the temple in Jerusalem without permission."

Artist Unknown (public domain)

For me Jesus looked like an ordinary kid – a somewhat bold, rebellious one at that, not asking for forgiveness at all.

Pop's letter went on:

"The story ends in Luke 2:52 with our verse: 'And Jesus increased in wisdom and in stature and in favor with God and man.'
This is all we know of the next 16 years of His life till the time of His baptism and the beginning of His public teaching. In His

father's carpenter shop, in the home, in the little synagogue school, in His playtime with His friends, Jesus increased in the four-fold development of His life.

He increased "in wisdom" - in brain-power, in knowledge, sitting with the other Jewish boys in the school connected with the village synagogue, memorizing their one textbook, which we know as the Old Testament. As you know this is the history of their race, stories of their mighty prophets and rulers, the sacred poetry of the Psalms, the legal code of Moses and the glorious prophesies of the future - a marvelous library indeed.

He increased "in stature" - in size and physical strength. Working day by day by the side of His father in the carpenter shop, playing with other boys when the tasks of the day were over, and oftentimes climbing to the top of the hill just behind Nazareth whence one could see on a clear day to the distant Mediterranean.

He increased "in favor with man" - in popularity and social qualities. Others of the village liked to have Him about and to join their company and pleasure.

He increased "in favor" with God - in spiritual qualities. Ever faithful in His daily devotions and prayer, He became "the beloved Son, in whom I am well pleased."

Thus He became the four-square person, perfectly developed in BODY, MIND, SOCIAL

QUALITIES and SPIRIT. One might enlarge on these four parts of our nature almost indefinitely.

Now we can consider what are the two distinctive and peculiar meanings of the ring. First, all four parts of the ring are the same size. From this we draw this lesson that all these parts of our nature should be equally developed, so that we can become even as Jesus, the four-square person. If any side of the square becomes longer or shorter than the others, it is no longer a square. So we see at times boys and men with the body over-developed, as the big beefy center of a football team or a prizefighter with magnificent body but no other ability whatsoever. Or a boy standing at the head of his class or graduating from college at the age of 15 or 16 (or even less) but with poor physique and no ability to form or keep friendships. Or a woman who becomes a social butterfly, beautiful dancer, a hail-fellow-well-met, but with no ability to tackle the big jobs of life. Or the religious fanatic -- the monk who leaves the world, or in India the fakir who mistreats his body in many ways, selfishly seeking his own salvation but caring nothing for the needy world around. Each of these is over-developed along one particular line, but failing in the high ideal of the four-square person that Jesus surely was.

And the second distinctive meaning of the ring grows out of this. Not only are the four parts of the same size, but they must lie side by side to form a single harmonious whole. When the ring is apart, even though all four parts are still of the same size, it is useless as a ring, but is only a puzzle - a mighty hard one you will agree. It is not easy to put the parts together, as all know who have tried. This may take, with the ring, the labor of hours, if unaided.

In the greater task of our life, it requires all of us, with all our possible effort to become four-square, equally developed, but also to succeed in keeping the proper balance of all these parts and to make them fit together into a harmonious life, helping and reinforcing each other.

Jesus, even at the age of twelve, had accomplished this task to a marvelous degree. And even then He went on, increasing day-by-day in this four-fold development 'till He became the perfect person, our example and helper: Be ye therefore perfect even as your Father in heaven is perfect. I can do all things through Christ who strengtheneth me.

So if you write to me, you can put a small square after your signature to let me know that you remember the "message of the puzzle ring" and that you are day-by-day trying to make your life four-square, even like that of Jesus.

    Your pal,
    Pop Ferger □ "

This long letter, more than any of the others, explained his simple message -- just four words and all coming together.

But I still didn't quite get it.

I always wanted to know more about Pop's life and the connection of the puzzle ring to the four words. I wore my ring with great pride, often demonstrating how to put it back to its wearable form to anyone who might show interest. Yet I seldom spoke to anyone about the ring's representation of the four words and the symbolism of the whole man. I kept my Bible next to my bed with Pop's hand-written name and square and often read the passage about the boy Jesus in St. Luke 2:52. (See Appendix B.)

I began my journey to live by Pop's four-square message even though I didn't really understand it. I just accepted that Jesus was a good person – maybe the example I yearned for -- and that Pop's message of being well-rounded in mind, body, social qualities, and spirit might somehow help me better my life. But how?

Young Kitty and Henri

Chapter 4

Along Came Kitty

Miss Kathryn Matilda Reinbold, born in Pennsylvania, April 21, 1887, was then a five-foot, one-and-a-half-inch beauty with light brown hair and blue eyes who worked at the Home for Boys at Jamestown where Henri spent so much time.

On April 24, only a few days after her twenty-eighth birthday, Henri, never the classic romantic, wrote in his diary, "Tonight I proposed to her and it turned out well! Great!"

Apparently, somewhere between Rawalpindi and his return to New Jersey, he lost a little of his shyness.

The month of May was busy for them both. He wrote, "Had a walk with Kitty." At some point, Henri had bestowed on her the nickname "Kitty." A day later he noted, "Strolled with Kitty. Lots of things clearing up." Followed by, "Kitty was appointed today to the Punjab Mission." Henri was ordained as a Presbyterian minister May 27, 1915, and he and Kitty were married on the 21st of July.

How Henri met and married Kitty between early April and late July may seem strangely rushed. While Henri was at Princeton, Kitty, a farm girl from Allentown, Pennsylvania, was hired after secretarial training by the New Jersey Boys School. The head of the reformatory, a family friend of the Fergers from Chattanooga, made Kathryn (Katie) Reinbold his secretary. As part of her job, she read Henri's letters from India, finding them so interesting that when Pop came to visit his friend in 1913 she knew more about Henri than he knew about her.

Despite the dangers of World War I, a global military conflict that took place primarily in Europe between 1914 and 1918, the bride and groom went off to India. In his letters Henri spoke of the possibility of being sunk by submarines in the ocean weather that brought rough seas to their transit. Yet to his bride he spoke only encouraging words. Using his newly-adopted manner of addressing her, he said, "Kittydear, be patient. This route to Bombay does take a while, but don't let all the bouncing and your seasickness get you down. We'll be there soon. Eat some crackers and come along with me -- spend some time on deck."

On August 6, 1915, they landed in Calcutta and began their life's work together.

The weather in August was not unlike New York and New Jersey, hot, humid, clothes sticking to sweaty skin, but the noise and smells were different – odors of burning charcoal and cow patties filled the damp air.

Pop taught mathematics half-time at Forman Christian College in Lahore, the capital city of Punjab, and spent the remainder studying the difficult languages of Hindustani and Urdu with Kitty. Henri always gave Kitty credit that she learned these languages, originating from Sanskrit, more quickly than he did.

Henri had already served three years in the Indian culture, but this life was new to Kittydear. Put yourself in her shoes. She had done some research about India and knew of Henri's decision, yet haggling with merchants in the market, cooking, shopping, and entertaining foreigners was a heavy challenge that first year. Compared to what their life could have been in America in 1915, this new land was a cultural desert. The only entertainment from the world she'd known came from BBC radio and a few foreign language broadcasts. From their first days in India, the couple walked the line between their English and Indian friends. Henri said, "Kittydear, cultures are not easily portable, nor are they easily learned."

Henri quickly became accustomed to being called sahib (gentleman), and Kittydear, the gamer that she turned out to be, adjusted to being a memsahib (wife). Over the next years the two took up, as a team, the challenges of their life's work: educating and ministering to young men and women of India.

Women?

Right... women.

In a culture that undervalued them, Kitty pitched in to make a contribution to their lives. She cared about all young people, particularly those having trouble getting started in life. Her job as secretary to the head of the New Jersey boys school had exposed her to all the problems of troubled youth. In India women were bred to care for husbands, much as were slaves in other cultures. Working for the mother-in-law was expected. With that came drudgery, every dirty job, absolute obedience, and no opportunity to rise.

Kitty asked a lot of questions which Henri endeavored to answer.

"What percent of marriages are arranged?" She asked.

"I have no precise statistics to back this figure, but compared to the past when the number was 100%, the recent period has witnessed around 30% less." He was guessing.

"What is the most popular food in India?"

"Probably Masala Dosa which originated from the South. If you consider sweets, it is probably Rasgolla which, I'm told, came from West Bengal." He added, "Tastes do vary a great deal between North and South, East and West. India is more a continent than a country.

"How do they make it?"

"You'll have to ask one of our church women." Henri said.

Kitty kept the questions coming, "Why don't they eat beef? Why?"

"Kittydear, you must be careful of these questions, "It is their religion – Hinduism. Cows are sacred among Hindus, and they form the majority."

"I don't understand the caste system."

He answered, "It's an age-old system."

Kitty went on, "What does Shudras mean? Is it a caste?

"Shudras refer to a caste of people who normally do menial jobs, one notch above Parayas, the Untouchable.

"What is the 10th class in high school? What is the equivalent in USA?

"Freshman," He mumbled.

Boys and girls in India never went to the same school, if at all, so Kitty's personal mission became a school for girls.

When Henri learned that Kitty loved the outdoors as much as he, they began to camp and hike in the mountains north of Delhi. They fell in love with one of the most beautiful locations in the world, the famed Vale of Kashmir, located in the valley between the Great Himalayas and the Pir Panjal range. In 1917 they went there to continue their study of the Hindu languages.

In April 1921, while on a business trip to Lahore, Henri contracted typhoid fever. Doctors ordered him to recuperate in Kashmir. With Kitty at his side, Pop wrote several letters home describing the place; his father had them published in a local newspaper.

As it turned out, Kitty, a quick student of foreign languages, was also an excellent writer. Together they prepared the "Station Letters" sent regularly to the churches and other organizations that funded the couple's mission. But it was Kitty, as shown below, who wrote the masterful letters that brought to life the colors and wonders of the flora and fauna of Kashmir.

> "On the first day we rubbed our sleepy eyes at five o'clock in the morning, had tea and toast, and left our house by six o'clock, walking about a quarter mile to our *tongas* (a light two-wheeled horse-drawn vehicle). We covered forty-eight miles, most of it downhill.
>
> "We had quite a variety of scenery the first day, the road winding through beautiful forests of pine and white oak, then getting picturesque views of a wild rushing river many miles below us and our road cutting through the steep mountainside, sometimes passing through tunnels. For many miles, the latter part of the stage, the road followed closely along the river – a wild, whirling, rushing mass of water, seeming angry because it had to leave its beautiful valley of Kashmir.
>
> "On Tuesday we had toast and tea at five in the morning and after fourteen miles farther on we had our breakfast in a Mohammedan cemetery. While stopping there we were entertained by several bird friends – a couple of orioles came to call, dressed in

their best yellow and black; several mynas, which look like our robin, though without the red breast, called and did a lot of talking; two kinds of crows came with no good intentions, I fear. Graceful Mr. Dhyal, who very seldom goes about without his wife, thought we might like music with our meals and gave us several numbers."

"On the third day we covered thirty-one miles of wild, beautiful scenery, bold, lofty precipices on either side of the river, here and there gentler slopes covered with deodars, or little valleys with rice fields that looked like so many patch-work quilts, there being terraces of the bright green of rice nurseries, where the seed is sown and from which plants are taken for transplanting, then the terraces polka-dotted with the transplanted rice, other terraces filled with water, looking like patches of silver cloth, and brown patches – terraces of newly planted earth.

"The remaining sixteen miles we traveled that day were through beautiful forests of deodar (the most beautiful evergreen tree there is anywhere) and a tangle of ferns and flowers. All the way from Murree the roadside was bright with the brilliant red of the pomegranate blossoms, the lavender of the bush indigo, and the yellow of the barberry, and from Rampur (our last stopping place) were great patches of iris. In some places the hillsides and meadows were blue with them. I wanted to jump out of the *Tonga*. Farther on *the wheat fields had great splashes of red, which we found were poppies. Nature's gold pieces - buttercups - were scattered broadcast, and here and there in some shady nook were dainty lady slippers and enough Queens lace along the way for any Royal lady's gown."*

In 1917, now only 28 years old, Henri was appointed principal and president of the Christian Boys High School, with about 500 students at Dehra Dun located north of Delhi near the border of Nepal. There he remained until 1920, when at age 30, he was transferred to become president of the high school in Ludhiana where he remained until their first furlough in 1923. At each school he introduced the MBSQS message.

August 1924 found them on their return to India, plus infant son John, via England and Bombay. For the next two years, Henri completed his first film project in Lahore (his interest in photos was growing), and became a member of the India Council of Boy Scouts.

During 1928-1932 Pop's interest in Boy Scouts grew, and in October 1930 he was honored with the name "Vijaiji" (victor or winner) at a Boy Scout rally; the ji meaning it is an honorific title. Thereafter, in India, his nickname was Vijaiji, not Pop, as it was in America.

In 1932 they returned to America, and to make some money, Henri worked as a counselor at boys camps, spreading his MBSQS message.

Two years later he and Kitty left again for India by way of St. John, Newfoundland, and Gibraltar, arriving in July 1934 at Bombay and continuing to Fatahgarh, where he served for 15 years as principal and manager of the American Presbyterian Christian High School and also worked as a member of the St. John Ambulance Association. For his excellent work he received the Kaiser-i-Hind Silver

Medal from the British government for public service contributions during the war. (The Kaiser-i-Hind was a medal awarded by the British monarch between 1900 and 1947 to civilians of any nationality who rendered distinguished service in the advancement of the interests of the British Raj. (Wikipedia)).

Henri was recalled from the dangers of war by his church organization. In 1942, the war year before I met Pop, he and Kitty turned the Christian high school in Fatehgarh over to Mr. Ram, a temporary headmaster, joined 350 Americans aboard S.S. Wakefield, formerly the S.S. Manhattan, and sailed at 11:00 a.m. on the morning of February 20, 1942.

Zigzagging all the way, at night, in a ship darkened with blackout curtains covering all portholes, their vessel crossed the Equator. By March 3, 1942, they were off the Cape of Good Hope, where they marveled at the many albatross surrounding the ship. They felt much safer after a stop at Cape Town. Their ship joined a convoy of a cruiser and destroyer plus two planes to protect their ship during their next transit across the Atlantic and into South American waters.

Docking at Brooklyn Navy Yard on March 23, 1943 they began a two-year respite. Not one to be idle, Pop spent June, July, August, and September at various camps for boys.

One of those camps was Greenwood near Pittsburgh, where I met him that summer of 1943 and learned the message of the puzzle ring.

Author's Pre-teen Photo

Chapter 5
Measuring Growth

The new year of 1944 brought another letter from Pop. It outlined a self-appraisal process for the four-square life. Looking back, I'm sure it was just chance, but someone else might call it mental telepathy – I needed not only inspiration but lots of guidance to understand better what my puzzle ring really meant – what Pop was getting at when he said "rise." I didn't even know what appraisal meant. The letter opened with the usual salutation and square representing the four-square letters: MBSQS.

"Dear Lamba Singh ☐

"This is intended to be a self-appraisal, as explained below, to be made carefully and with prayer. Do not be hasty in this judgment of yourself. Aim high.

"BODY - Be physically strong.

Participate in regular games or exercise, get plenty of regular sleep, no cigarettes, well balanced food diet with but little eating between meals. Good health, absence of bad physical habits, shoulders back and chest well out and abdomen in ...

"MIND - Mentally awake

Make a real effort at school and get good grades or better in schoolwork. Have regular habits of reading and study; reading solid books, magazines and papers of travel, biography, current affairs and the like (comic sections and sporting pages do not count for or against.)

"SOCIAL QUALITIES -- Do others like you?

Are your companions of the right sort? Do you meet others easily? Are you faithful in your friendships and their obligations? Do you do your full share in the chores of the home (such as garden, kitchen work, chickens - if anything - cleaning of your own room and making your own bed) without grumbling or being reminded? Are you neat in appearance – clothing, hair, fingernails, etc?

"SPIRIT -- Morally straight

Have regular devotions (such as Morning Watch); readings of the Bible and at least occasionally religious books and magazines; regular habits of prayer; regular attendance at least two of these – Sunday School, church service, young peoples' group; regular use of some part of your income (pocket money, earnings, etc.) for some benevolent purpose (as for your church and Sunday school). Membership in the church and a real share in its work – do you look on it as YOUR church?

"Please think over each of these four sections, grading yourself on the basis of 25 as perfect for each part, or a total of 100 for the four. This will show where you feel your weakness is and where you need to work most to make yourself the four-square man like your Master. Talk over your score if you wish with some adult whom you fully trust such as your father or mother, your Sunday school teacher or pastor and ask for their help and suggestions. Remember that we read that 'Jesus INCREASED" in each of these; so can you!

> *"I would be glad for you to send me what you feel to be your score on each part, and for any comment or question you wish to ask.*
>
> *Your Pal,*
Pop ☐"

My first reaction was to disregard his self-appraisal crap; I was still out of sorts with the world.

A few days later I picked it up and read the steps, again and again. After reading Pop's letter a second time, I thought my parents would do well to read it -- it wasn't crap. But I decided not to show it to them. A tan'n on my backside would probably be my reward.

The self-appraisal steps were simply worded and not tricky in any way. I did want to rise – to become a four-square person. It couldn't hurt to take the test – no one else would know.

I won't tell you my score.

Forget that, I will tell.

Suffice that it was not very high, but at that time I didn't have a very good image of myself. I was weak in Mind – schoolwork didn't interest me. My grades were low; I didn't put in the time. I'd rather play – especially outdoors away from Mom. I did like to read sometimes with a flashlight under the covers. Pop wanted me to aim high; I gave myself 10 points.

Body was better, though I smoked and I was skinny. My diet was not always balanced, not because of my mother's cooking but because I set pins on two lanes in a bowling alley after school, frequently until after midnight, and often skipping meals. However I did like all sports – especially basketball. I gave myself 25, then dropped it to 15 because I knew smoking was bad for me.

Social Qualities was a real downer – still very bashful – I think some of the girls liked me, but I was so shy I couldn't hold a conversation. I gave myself 5 points.

I thought I was reasonably spiritual but not into it as much as many of my church friends – 10 points.

My total count was 40, so I didn't talk it over with anyone – no dad, no adult – too shy.

I did ask myself, "Where am I going? How can I improve?"

My pre-teen photo shows a bold and sassy kid but shortly after that, I became a Pittsburgh Press paperboy. Each morning, while folding a bag full for delivery, I read the headlines. The world began to open. India showed up on the front page almost as much as World War II, which, for America, had been underway almost three years. I knew a lot about that war. I even played games in our basement with my buddies. We pretended to be bomber or fighter pilots, or sailors on ships shooting down Japanese Kamikazes, or soldiers in hand-to-hand combat.

America got into the war after Japan bombed Pearl Harbor. Now our men were fighting against the Nazi Germans of Europe and the Japanese in the South Pacific, and dying. Most cartoons of Germans looked like Hitler – he wore a short square mustache under his nose. The Japanese cartoons showed ruthless soldiers stabbing people with bayonets.

Because Pop's mission was in India, I read every newspaper article about that country. I learned that a Christ-like man named Mahatma Gandhi was leading a non-violent revolt to gain India's independence from Britain, another country I knew little about. Pictures of Gandhi showed him as a skinny little man with a bald head and big nose who wore glasses and dressed in simple homespun cloth (I learned much later that his white sheet was the sign of a Nationalist). I wondered how he could cause so much trouble.

Pop never mentioned the war in his letters. I suppose that was because as a missionary he had to be neutral or at least sympathetic to India's causes. I read that soldiers with names like *Sikhs, Punjabis, Dogras, Gurkas, Garthwalis*, and *Pathans*, all known for their bravery, had repelled the invasion of India by Japanese forces and served alongside the British in Europe.

I thought about enlisting. Maybe the Army would send me to India. But fourteen was too young.

Since I first learned about India from Pop, I wished to know more about that mystery place and its people. He promised to explain its complex culture once he was settled in his work.

At various times he did send me pictures and gifts of a cultural nature. One that I prized most seemed to be no more than a long rag the length of a tablecloth. Using his instructions I carefully wrapped that single colorful cloth around my head until I mastered the turban headdress. Pretending I was a *Sikh* or a *Gurka*, I secretly practiced in front of a mirror.

Sometime after my fifteenth birthday, I thumb tacked a Rand McNally world map on the wall near my bed. To me it looked like the humans had inhabited the globe on several large islands surrounded by vast amounts of water. India was a very big country with lots of poor people. Without realizing, I was developing a world view.

When people asked me, "What's your plan for your life?" I answered, "See the world."

My self-appraisal was lousy and I wondered if I was ready. On the other hand, I realized that others judged me, so what's wrong with judging myself? I thought, *better work on my weaknesses. But where to start?*

Some high school kids in my neighborhood told me that just like at Overbrook Elementary and Junior, at Carrick High all the male teachers wore neckties and the female teachers had their hair done – but the difference was that they were mean people who kept kids back a grade if they failed.

Terror!

Author as Teenager

Chapter 6

Growing Up

After the chance meeting with Pop in 1943, my years passed like one of John Wayne or Gene Autry's silver bullets, and with that I began to change -- growing up, I suppose.

Promotion to high school was not as fearsome as the older kids from the neighborhood said it would be. Carrick sat at the crest of our mountain and to get there, rain or snow, the kids who lived in Overbrook had to climb to the top and slide back to the bottom at the end of the day.

Yah, yah, I know. Lots of parents tell their kids how tough it was in their day, but in this case, trust me, it's all true.

In 1945, still shy at 15, I carefully began to show off my puzzle ring. Pop's message about living the four-square life and becoming a man crept back into my mind.

I wanted to be a man, whatever that was, and I was trying not to be like my father, drunk and not caring about his family.

Where does one start?

*****

Understanding Pop's puzzle ring message varies among young people, who grow up at different rates. Some say girls mature earlier than boys. Secondly, boys and girls of today's generation are often just living in the moment, not yet ready to take on long-range plans for their future.

What should we expect of ourselves? Sooner or later we have to face the future. What we don't want to happen, later in life, to hear ourselves say, "If only I had been jarred by somebody and forced to settle down. Along the way we might trip and fall. If that happens, the deal is, get up and get on your feet.

The first step is to stop blaming; I found that, after my dad left, I was full of anger. It doesn't help.

Then there was jealousy. One of my grade school classmates was a friend named Freddie Slater. His father was an undertaker. On rainy days we sometimes went inside their house to play, and it was on one of those occasions that we ended up in Freddy's bedroom to get a toy or something. As I looked around his room, I compared it with my own. Mine was in a cubbyhole; his was an entire room with dressers and a desk. His clothes were hung in a closet, spic and span. He even had drawers where his pants, shirts, underwear, and sweaters were all lined up neatly. He had many of each. I had only two trousers hanging over a hook and one drawer with a few undershorts. I became instantly jealous of Freddie. We weren't poor, but Freddy's family was certainly better off than mine. Although we remained buddies, I never went to Freddy's house again.

More important is to know our own weaknesses as shown by measuring growth and to select your worst area(s) to concentrate.

I knew I needed to improve my mind and social qualities. Also, during the years from 15 through 17, I had no leadership characteristics at all, and probably wouldn't have wanted to show them even if I did – I was too shy.

Pop Ferger's message was there, in my mind, but I hadn't listened very well. I had to learn from my mistakes.

I was prone to follow others and got caught stealing a pack of cigarettes from a local drug store. Leaders of the micro-gang I had joined urged me to do it, so to prove I wasn't chicken, I stupidly did it – and got caught. I felt terrible and embarrassed. I knew it was a dumb thing for me to do. But strangely my shame was less about being caught by the owner than because one of my female classmates who lived on my street in Overbrook saw me kicked out of the store. Fortunately the owner didn't call the police or I might have spent some time in juvenile hall.

I was still a loner. Despite being a good worker, I didn't fit in. A joiner I was not. I avoided cliques.

Other things happened before I began to put the MBSQS message into action. One of my schoolmates brought a bottle of cheap red wine to the basement of the school. We were caught drinking, sent to the principal's office, and expelled three days from school. But that punishment was nothing compared to the fate I expected. I thought my mom would rip my bare butt severely with my own belt as she had done before. But she surprised me: She didn't fly into the fury I deserved and expected. After hearing the story she said, "Well, this won't be the last time you'll have to make a choice. Next time do the right thing."

And she was right. Growing up is all about making better choices and learning from bad choices. For me, Pop's puzzle ring message was a guide to learning how to do that. However, letter writing came after working, basketball, baseball, tennis, and music.

In school, basketball finally claimed my athletic interest. During my awkward stage in elementary and junior high, I barely made sports teams. The worst embarrassment was always being picked last. I barely made the ninth grade basketball team and even then was given only half a uniform. I think it was the shirt, because that's all that was left over. Sometime between ninth and tenth grades, as my *farmor* (Swedish grandmother) predicted, I grew to be taller than six feet – actually six feet three inches -- and I came into my own.

Basketball became my life. I spent most of my spare time shooting baskets and playing one-on-one against my little brother Gordon. We even built a hoop on a telephone pole under a streetlight so we could shoot or play games after dark, rain or snow. Mom had to come and get us to eat or do chores. For us basketball was like a drug. We were drawn to it like fish to the ocean; we couldn't help ourselves. The sport was perfect for two tall Swedish-American kids.

Because we were in lean financial years, I had to contribute to household expenses. We needed money; dad didn't pay any child support. Most nights I worked until midnight or later, jumping two lanes at the local bowling alley. Other times I worked similar hours as a soda jerk at Liggetts Drug Store in downtown Pittsburgh. I was constantly sleepy because I went to bed tired and woke up still tired. I often arrived late for school and received many after-school detentions as my penalty. On days when there was a basketball game, I would, following my detention, and to the cheers of the crowd, run onto the court well into the first quarter. I earned a reputation for being late, and the nickname "Sleepy" went with it. It should have been "Bored."

Seeing cute girls hanging on the arms of the star athletes and drinking cherry coke from the fountain at Johnny's Drug Store was part of my motivation. I not only made the high school basketball team, but in my senior year became a starter.

The cherry coke and girls never materialized, probably because of my shyness. I avoided girls because I didn't know what to say. I didn't even ask a girl to the senior prom.

Shortly after graduation, life for me in Pittsburgh came to an end. I could feel the pull of foreign places. World War II was over but, for the boys of Carrick, military service, our rite of passage, remained. During the years of World War II, 1941-45, almost all the boys left school as soon as they were old enough, often without graduating,

We didn't wear love of country on our sleeves, but most of the boys in my graduating class went into the armed forces. I didn't join immediately, but the mystery of what was beyond Overbrook, the thoughts of another woman in my life besides my mother and a house and street different than 2038 Dartmore began to excite my imagination. Stepping into the unknown felt comfortable, even though I had no idea what my life's work might be. My mother encouraged me to go to college. Grandmother Sadie thought I should become an ordained pastor.

Not wanting to work in a steel mill or coal mine, I took a job as a stock boy in downtown Pittsburgh in the Grant Building and began attending night college. That routine of school and work soon took its toll in boredom. I wanted to move on, to see foreign places, and hopefully India.

One grey, dreary, soot-covered, snowy day in the winter of 1949, walking along Diamond Street, I spied the shoeshine man. I don't know why, but I always envied those who could afford to have their shoes shined. I gathered enough courage to ask how much.

"Fifty cents."

That was about all the money I had, but I climbed into the chair anyway. When he finished, I couldn't take my eyes off the shine. I walked along Diamond Street with my head down, admiring the toes. When I lifted my head, I was standing in front of a storefront with a big sign that said, "Join the Navy or Marine Corps. See the World!" Everyone in that recruiting office had spit-shined shoes.

My mind jumped to Pop's message: Mind, Body, Social Qualities, and Spirit. I was headed nowhere but knew I needed an opportunity and a change. I instantly made my first life decision. I said to myself, "That's what I want to do!" I walked boldly up to a recruiter and said, "I want to enlist in the Navy."

That night, when I told my mom what I had done, Isabel gave me a big hug and said, "You did the right thing... now follow your heart. If you fall down, get up and get on your feet."

Equipped with Pop's MBSQS message as a model, wearing my puzzle ring, and armed with mom's blessing, I set off on April 9, 1949, to see the globe. I hugged my mother and climbed aboard the bus heading west. My thoughts were about the mysteries of the other world places I longed to see. Being a sailor would solve that problem.

As the Greyhound sped west, I took out a pencil and paper and began my first letter. It would be to my mother. My intention was to write a lengthy letter and get it mailed when we transferred in Chicago, but I didn't finish it in time. Instead I settled on a simple thank you to my mom. "Thanks for everything in my life, Mom. I promise to keep you posted about the Navy." Thinking she might not be able to get along financially, I told her, "I'll send you something from my paychecks -- the recruiters said I'll get about $85.00 a month."

I finished another letter, this one to Pop Ferger. I told him where I was and what I was doing. By now it had been six years since I had met him. He was in his 39th year of missionary work in India. My journey to become a four-square person had been herky-jerky. I did some things well, but looking back, I was not proud of my rebellious bad-boy stage. My score using Pop's grading sheet remained about 40.

Rain lay in puddles the day I arrived at the Great Lakes Naval Training Center near Chicago and the wind, fresh off Lake Michigan, reminded me of ocean smells. I pulled the collar of my jacket tight around my neck to ward off the morning chill. Intending to look calm, even tough, I walked with an imaginary swagger practiced at home in front of a mirror. Boys from Overbrook who served in the Navy during World War II called it looking "salty."

Beneath the swagger my heart pounded. For the first time in my life I felt free. I was finally on my own.

A guard, an emblem sewn on the right sleeve of his blue uniform that looked like a chicken resting on two broken fence rails, pointed to a large brick structure and said, "Report to Building One – and you better drop that walk – you're only a boot."

The building looked a lot like Carrick High School, concrete blocks and lots of windows. I was told to stand next to a guy wearing farmers' boots and coveralls who smelled like he looked, just off the farm. Other recruits looked about my age, 17 or 18. Some wore leather jackets, others mackintoshes, and one guy even wore a suit and tie with a handkerchief in his coat pocket. I eased away from the farmer and stood among about 60 others all huddled together listening to a short, stocky, bald guy who said, "Okay, listen up. Yunz can call me Chief Godin." He had the body language I expected of all sailors -- a cocky swing of his shoulders and arms and an arrogant walk. When he wasn't using his hands, he hooked his fingers into the waistband of his trousers; I suppose it was a habit after years when sailor's pants had no pockets. He pointed to the patch on his left arm that looked like a bomb between two wings. He simply said,

"Aviation ordnance man," then added, "Leave your enlistment orders here, then follow me to the barber. Afterwards yunz'll go to the barracks and take a shower before going to bed. Tomorrow morning, bright and early, you will fold the clothes you're wearing and put them into a box to be sent back home.

"OK, another thing," Godin said. "There will be about 60 boots in Company 127. Get to know one another. Yunz'll be smelling each others armpits before this is over, that is if yunz make it – and some of yunz won't.

"Okay, one more thing. This ain't going to be no picnic. One twenty seven's gonna be a good company, the best. Yunz're in the Navy now and I ain't your mother, but if yunz got problems, tell me. I want to know what's going on, okay?"

Right away I knew Chief Godin was from Pittsburgh because he had already used the word "yunz" seven times. Pittsburgheze mixed a local patois with specific words used only in certain sections of Western Pennsylvania.

Every sailor remembers the sound of thunder on their first morning in the service. At the end of the barracks, rolling a broom handle around the inside of a corrugated trash can, stood Chief Godin.

"Drop your cocks and grab your socks, ladies! OK. Fun's over. Navy life begins today." That was followed by something I heard leaders say over and over again in my Navy career, "Get up, get on your feet!"

Just as I hit my head on the top bunk, one of my fellow boots said, "This is bullshit."

Though I'm a regular guy who had done my share of dumb things during my teens and beyond, I never picked up cussing as a habit. My *farmor* (Swedish for grandmother) once told me that cussing was something people adopted who were uneducated and unsure of themselves. She said that some people just used those words as an expression that gave no more clarity than a simple "yes" or "no" but identified the speaker as someone who needed to show a veneer of toughness. It's not that I didn't know all the words, but I never took ownership and was never comfortable with them. Usually I compromised by saying "frig." That way I felt like I was one of the boys even though I hadn't really cussed.

Chief Godin waited for the moans and groans and cussing to subside, then added, "Go to the head. That's Navy talk for the bathroom. Then get back in line by height in the middle of the barracks, two lines. We'll march to the mess hall, eat, and get your gear. Hustle! Move out, boots!"

"I'm in the real Navy!" I said to myself.

We began to learn every aspect of Navy war-fighting at the basic sailor level. First came marching "One, two, one two, hup-two-three-four. Hup, two..." The drone of cadence echoed across the grinder barren of trees and immaculately cleaned of even the smallest scrap of paper or cigarette butt by boot sailors.

Then came history, survival swimming, weapon firings. Learning the ship from stem to stern came next. Tying knots. Engineering. The sessions were repeated every day from early 'til late.

"Smitdorf!"

"Yo. Hey, I got a letter. Let me through!"

Once a day the petty officer in charge of mail would shout "mail call," and we would all rush to surround him with expectations of a letter from home.

Sometimes the sea of bodies would part to let a man wade through; other times the letter was passed hand over hand to the back of the crowd. If the guy wasn't present for some reason, a buddy took it for him or the mail petty officer left it for him on his rack.

Mail call was the primary way recruits stayed connected to our parents, families, and girlfriends. Some had enough money to make phone calls, but most of us were dead broke and postage was cheaper. Holding it away from the guys, he would reach in the pouch, bring out each piece one at a time, often agonizingly slow, and call out the name. "Pokorski. You got two and --" the mail man held it close to his nose, "This one has perfume on it."

That always brought a lot of smart remarks from the guys, but inside I suspected each had the same touch of jealousy I felt. I yearned to have a girl back home who would write to me.

"Milligan."

"Yo, let me through." Milligan pushed his way to the front, took the single letter, held it to his nose, then pushed his way to the perimeter.

I missed my mom but I didn't miss her. You know that feeling? It wasn't as if we didn't get along -- it was just time for me to get away. She raised my brother and me alone, a single mom. She was tough, always on me for something, but I was already lonesome and would like to have heard my name called. I had promised to write and did so on the way to Great Lakes, but I hadn't written since nor received one letter from her.

When it was all over, there were always several guys who didn't get mail; their disappointment showed on their faces as they returned to their bunks to wait for chow call. I knew the feeling, that is, until I heard my name called. "Yo," I shouted and pushed my way through the remaining sailors.

My mother's letter brought me up to date about her new job. She had met a man and would probably marry him. She praised me for being so prompt with my first letter and reminded me that after serving my four-year hitch, I would be eligible for college or other training through veteran's benefits such as the GI Bill. She was already looking ahead at what my life's work might be after the Navy.

I had put little thought about my future beyond the Navy -- it seemed so far off. All I saw was four years of wonderful travel aboard warships. Boot camp was tough and many guys wanted to quit. But for me it was a good fit. I liked the Navy. I had little time for a self-evaluation using MBSQS, but I did it anyway. In my mind I improved to about sixty percent, and although still ashamed, I sent it to Pop. "Maybe something will happen to improve my score – maybe the Navy will help me improve."

The stimulation I was looking for it came as an answer to my self-appraisal of the four-square life.

"Dear Lamba Singh □

"Do not be hasty in this judgment of yourself. Think deeply about the four foundations and like Jesus, live and rise by the four-square life: MIND, BODY, SOCIAL QUALITIES, and SPIRIT.

I would be glad for you to send me your scores on each part and any comment or question you may wish to ask. But don't give up.

Your Pal,
Pop □ *"*

When I finished reading his short letter, I reflected that maybe he knew something I didn't – that some event would determine what I did in life. Little did I know how soon that would happen.

"What will be the tests to determine the true greatness of India in the 1950's?"

A typical question from Henri Ferger to his students

Chapter 7
Teaching Boys in India

Henri's puzzle ring message wasn't meant just to challenge American boys. He circled the globe eight times, including visits to such out-of-the-way places as Timbuktu. Wherever he traveled he spoke to anyone who would listen about his notion of the whole person, the four-square life.

The dominant place he took his message was, of course, to the Christian mission in India. There, in order to carry out their assignment, Henri and Kitty had to explain how Mind, Body, Social Qualities, and Spirit (MBSQS) might be useful in the many cultures of that land -- multiple languages, long history, many religions, different diet, and very complex social and political issues.

Their primary responsibility was the academic curriculum that supported the needs of their students; at the same time, they kept their American church sponsors aware of progress including many of the day-to-day happenings.

That both Henri and Kitty typed very well helped in corresponding to churches and Sunday schools back home that collected pennies and nickels to support them. They both contributed regularly to the "Station Letters," painting very detailed pictures of life in India, a country where, Henri once said, "More people can travel in the same amount of space without seeming to mind the discomfort than any other country in the world." Their letters were forthright, telling the American folks that a few of their students were Christians but most were not, with more Hindus than Muslims. They explained the term hereditary estates. Graft, bribery, cliques, rivalries, priest-craft, and immorality were major vices among princes and officials and all very appalling to Henri and Kitty.

They also wrote about the caste system based solely on birth that predetermined a person's social position and work opportunity. The two agreed that castes (in rank order: Brahmin, Chatra, Shudras, and Parayas) amount to the denial of the right of universal brotherhood.

Henri saw the problems as Muslims and Hindus hating each other and business managers of both religions labeling people from birth with a caste. They also saw the subjugation of Indian women as part of a larger issue. MBSQS was meant to give people a way to break through the barriers. Their solution was their mission: Christianity, Boy Scouts, and better education, not necessarily in that order.

When invited to petitioners' or teachers' homes, Henri would speak Hindi, eat with his fingers, dress in Indian clothes with his shirt tail outside, baggy pajama pants and a vest with bright colors, and wear a hat, always. Kitty, when appropriate and invited, went with him wearing, occasionally, a sari, considered one of the most alluring dresses in the world.

Both served as experienced Christian missionaries and, from the descriptions in their letters, the two seemed very fit for their roles. Visualize the two settled into chairs in the middle of the high-vaulted living room of their mission house. Kitty, round-faced and motherly, looked more suited for baking pies in the hills of Pennsylvania where, in fact, they intended to live when they retired to the States. Henri, a tall, trim man with a full head of white hair and mustache would no longer be mistaken as the athletic academic from Princeton that he was when he first came to the Punjab and joined the mission in 1910.

Coming and going amongst them were a houseboy, a cook, and a maid. Indian family incomes hovered around 100 rupees per month, about US $14, and most lived in one- or two-room houses made of mud, straw, and cow dung. Many couldn't afford to send their children even to a free school because they earned money tending cattle. Henri and Kitty helped a few by bringing them into their house.

Henri's church sat in the middle of the trees, far from the road, an old structure of weatherworn bricks surrounded by flowers, shrubs, and a brick wall topped with a large bell. A plaque on the wall commemorated the first pastor who had it constructed about 80 years before. Solid marble tile floors supported a carved altar with brass ornaments. Bible inscriptions, written in the florid Arabic script of the Urdu language, outlined the chancel and the side doors.

The small church, with its straight-backed pews, could seat about a hundred, and on most Sundays it was fairly full. Students and visitors complemented local members. Four or five well-to-do families drove cars to church; everyone else, members of the lower classes, walked.

Henri, who abhorred castes, would often tell all, as he waved at the walls, "There's no caste or class in here." Rather than shifting to the modern style of individual communion cups, the congregation drank wine from one unhygienic but beautiful old brass chalice. At issue was the symbolism of overcoming inter-caste eating restrictions, a problem that persisted in many churches.

Kitty made sure the ritual of teatime was observed every day at 4 p.m. in their home. It was a tradition she and Henri had learned from the British, and it became a ritual that continued all their lives. Anyone could come right on in, regardless of class.

Throughout their time in India, Henri and Kitty were assigned highly responsible jobs. Henri continued his quest to influence boys to adopt MBSQS in their rise to manhood. He was well-suited for that work; he had changed over time from the bashful young man he was when he left Princeton to become a gregarious person who loved to travel and talk to all kinds of people wherever he went.

Kitty, equally easy to know and very much the lady, continued her earlier work by starting, wherever they were assigned, a school for girls otherwise denied education. Not as technical as a regular school, Kitty focused on useful skills such as nursing, cooking, and gardening.

Henri was always a vigorous man, never spending much time sitting around, nor did Kitty.

He saw himself as a father figure, a moral compass who in every school organized a list of several do's and never-do's of which he reminded his students regularly, such as:

- **Always redeem a pledge.**
- **Never fail a friend.**
- **Never lie.**
- **Never cheat.**

He and Kitty respected Hindu, Buddhist, Jain, and Muslim religions but struggled to teach boys who, with different religions, didn't always like each other, that regardless of religion, we all must stand before the same God. That was where MBSQS and the Boy Scouts became important, for they emphasized that "Spirit" is just one part of the equation.

Of course the Fergers made it clear that MBSQS should be used only if it worked for their students as individuals. At no time was there pressure to change, for they were essentially non-judgmental: Henri and Kitty only wanted Hindu and Muslim boys to see their opportunities and take advantage of them.

What was Henri like in the classroom?

The Message of the Puzzle Ring

He was a strict disciplinarian who would also have his boys over for tea and biscuits. He was, in short, a much-loved teacher and administrator who connected with everyone on a human level.

To build morale in his schools he developed a motto "DYB-DOB" which he instilled everywhere he worked. It stood for "Do Your Best – (we'll) Do Our Best." He encouraged the boys to do something every day to improve themselves and help others.

Of course the three R's (reading, writing, and arithmetic) were the foundation of each school's formal curriculum. The message MBSQS was always a part of his less-formal program, especially when working with the Boy Scouts with their emphasis on outdoor education: ecosystems, plant, animal identification, including birds and fish other wildlife.

Of special interest was self-determination for India and the caste system. These issues were discussed throughout India during the entire period of the Fergers' service. It was regularly given space in newspapers and conversation. But Henri and Kitty, because of their missionary status, could not comment openly, even though they stood squarely in support of democracy and the abolishment of the castes.

Although unable to argue the issues himself, Henri challenged his students to think about preparing to participate in an independent India and to even become leaders in India's future.

One technique was to assign an essay topic, in this case: "What will be the tests to determine the true greatness of India in the 1950's?" Each student in the 10th class would write an essay from which Henri, with the help of other teachers, would select the best of the lot.

Here are several responses from the best, in their own words.

Indian Student #1:

"Before discovering the subject, there arises an important question concerning the greatness of India... What should be the race, caste, and religion of India in the 1950's. This is a problem that we should leave for better minds to solve. But in my opinion it is nearly impossible that there can be one religion or caste in India. But India cannot reach its greatness unless every individual thinks himself to be Indian, no matter whether he be a Hindu or Mohammedan."

"There is another equally important thing for the greatness of India. This is unity among the people of the country, a thing without which we cannot improve in any way. And if India cannot have this, it should not expect to be great. Love is also one of the essential things for the people of India to see on the stage of its true greatness.

"Another important thing that India requires to show its greatness is education. Now-a-days schools are merely clerk producing machines. India cannot be benefited by good education until it is made compulsory at least for the primary section, and this cannot be done unless there is free education... "

Indian Student #2:

"Before thirty years are past India will have gotten Home Rule. India sleeping as she has been will have spent a good number of her beautiful morning hours. By that time she will be prominent in the eyes of others and she will stand *as a giant before the world. So by the time India will be on one of the highest steps of the ladder of progress but her greatness will be attained in a different way. I do not desire that she will be like Japan and other countries of Europe are today.*

"India by that time will not remain only a geographical term. There will be real unity, which can be seen, even now in the primary stages. Brahmans will not abhor Shudras. There will be no hatred between a Hindu and a Muslims... "

Indian Student #3:

"I am sure that every one will admit that a man possessing spiritual power is truly a great man. A nation is composed of people and so a nation spiritually great should be looked upon as truly a great nation. It is quoted in our holy Shastas that a man might acquire what is called wisdom, wealth, etc., yet he has got nothing if he does not possess spiritual power."

Thus Henri tried to capture the minds of his students, encouraging hundreds of Indian and Muslim young adults to deal with national issues.

The Christian school near the church, the first high school in Fatehgarth, was for all religious groups, Hindus, Muslims, and Sikhs. The school compound was, as anyone who knew Henri Ferger would expect, orderly and purposeful. Well-dressed students sipped tea at a clean little stand.

One could imagine the incredible culture shock that most of the village children must have experienced on their arrival at Henri's school. Straight from mud huts to bricks and plumbing. Their narrow village with their rigid society of caste and family would be replaced at Henri's school by morning prayers, Boy Scouts, the 4-H, and evening Bible studies. It would be hard for a graduate from Pop's institution to return to the village. But it was either that or join the competition for scarce jobs in cities of incredibly large populations. Many took their education and entered government service.

Henri's hope was that some of his charges, over the many years he served as principal of schools, would go on to make a difference after independence.

Sailor

Chapter 8
Brig Time on Bread and Water

New sailors at boot camp are required to undress, except for under shorts, fold and pack their civilian clothes into a box addressed to their home, then carry it to the mailroom. It's their last vestige of civilian life until the end of the enlistment contract.

My first full day in the Navy was spent running back and forth to stand in long lines where we were handed GI gear -- everything we would need in our new life: pillows, sheets, underwear, towels, bell-bottom trousers, white hats, flat hats, dungaree pants, stencils, little ditty bags, big sea bags, boots, socks, and leggings.

Using our newly-found marching skill, we were led to a small auditorium with bleacher-style seats. A tall chief petty officer with salt-and-pepper hair wearing a single-breasted khaki coat with gold buttons stood in the center of the stage, calmly waiting for us to take our seats. His wrinkled face, streaked like a piece of weathered driftwood, sat on a neck and body so skinny he looked like an underfed Irish farmer during the potato famine. "No talking," he said. But a low hum floated among us as we adjusted to the rock-hard benches.

"Ok, we'll get started. Gentleman, I'm Chief Taylor. I'm a boatswain's mate, the best damn rate in the Navy and also your instructor for this class in seamanship. Gentlemen. Settle down.

"Of course you all know who John Paul Jones was –- he's called 'The Father of the American Navy' even though he was born in Scotland and didn't come to this country until 1773. They say that, unlike you, John Paul was a sailor from the time he was a baby. At the outbreak of the American Revolution, he equipped a small fleet and began harassing English shipping. He was known for surprise attacks and daring strikes that brought not only fear and terror into British hearts but also European sympathy for the American cause. He is, by the way, buried at the chapel at the United States Naval Academy in Annapolis, Maryland, where, I'm told, a few of you may wish to attend. I wish you good luck – it ain't easy.

"Today," Chief Taylor continued, "our ships are made of steel and powered by steam or diesel engines. We have many different types, some small and some very large. The smallest might be a submarine or a minesweeper or even a small landing craft. The largest would be an aircraft carrier, which could draw as much as 45,000 tons, or our battleships. In between we have cruisers and destroyers and oilers. You all have been issued a copy of *The Bluejackets Manual*. I want you to read it every night before you go to bed, learn what's in it. It's the bible of the U.S. Navy sailor."

Every time I began to drift off, Chief Taylor seemed to come up with something interesting.

"Now, a little serious talk," continued the chief. "Who knows the difference between a ship and a boat? Anybody? What? No one knows the difference? OK, a ship is generally large and a boat is small. We chiefs, because we run the Navy and we know everything, ha, ha, always say a boat is any vessel small enough to be hoisted and carried aboard a ship. Another distinction is that boats generally have only one compartment, but the interior of a ship's hull has many watertight compartments. This is because we don't want the ship to go down if just one compartment gets flooded.

"Now memorize this: Fire is your worst enemy. It killed more sailors in WWII than all the bullets and Kamikazes. That's why we spend so much time standing careful watches and learning how to fight fires. Tomorrow you will fight your first fire. You must fight them aggressively. It's your duty!"

Boot camp wasn't easy, but having learned to keep my mouth shut at home around my mom, the chiefs seemed to leave me alone. I even made the special drill team – you know the ones that entertain visitors by spinning their rifles and marching precisely to the beat of drums and bugles. I boxed in a couple of company competitions, and I did well – didn't knock anyone out and didn't get too banged up, mostly because I was taller than my opponents.

After boot camp I was sent to a specialty school to learn about electricity and electronics. One day while I was playing a pickup basketball game in the base gym, I was discovered by Coach McCann. He asked me if I would try out for his base basketball team. I felt like an old salt the day I showed up at the gym to show off my stuff. I changed into gym shorts and shoes and joined about 25 or 30 others who were invited to make the team. The coach was a civilian, a leftover from the war years when military sports teams were the best in the country. At that time the Great Lakes football team was made up of college All-Americans and pros, and the team competed against the best college and professional teams. The basketball teams were equally good.

With the war over, very few of the best basketball players in the country joined the Navy. Our team was made up of former high school players, a few officers who had already graduated from college, and Negroes who, for the first time, were permitted to play.

African Americans, as they later were called, had participated in every major U.S. war, but it wasn't until July 26, 1948, well after World War II, that President Harry S. Truman issued Executive Order 9981 officially ending racial segregation in all branches of the armed forces.

Although President Truman commanded an end to segregation, he permitted local commanders to implement his order at such time they deemed it appropriate. This "weasle-wording" permitted some military commands to continue racial segregation four more years. It would not be until well into the Korean War that the last segregated African-American unit would be abolished.

The Civil Rights Movement began about 1945 by using the federal courts to attack those laws. It wasn't until the winter of 1950 that I experienced Jim Crow first hand. I had never been around dark-skinned kids before, but when we played three on three, winners stay up, skin color didn't matter - only talent and winning counted. A couple of the southern guys who had been around black people all their lives went to the coach and complained.

"They try'n out for the team?" one asked

"Yup," Coach McCann responded.

"We have to play with them?" another asked.

"If you and they make the team, you will."

"I ain't play'n with no niggers."

"Suit yourself," coach said; "If you won't play with them, you may as well turn in your uniform right now. Go to sea."

A couple of them did, just walked off. One called the coach a nigger lover behind his back.

One of the white guys said to the complainers, "Hey, a couple of those guys are good ball players."

"No never mind. I don't play with niggers."

"Suit yourself."

I heard later he ended up on the USS Castor, AKS-1, a Navy transport loaded with black sailors. I wondered how he got along -- probably one of those guys who sat at a separate all-white table in the mess hall.

"You gonna play with them if you make the team?" I asked a guy from Erie, Pennsylvania.

"Sure," he answered. "First of all I'm gonna make this team because I heard the coach say that Annapolis recruits from here, and I haven't seen any big men any better than me -- and second, I don't care if a ball player is blue, green, or brown. You care?"

I didn't answer him right away, but I was already thinking about Pop's message. "HE (Jesus) increased 'in favor with God and man' - in popularity and social qualities. Others of his village liked to have HIM about and to join in their company and pleasure."

I responded, "Nah – skin color doesn't bother me."

Looking back, I learned a lot about how to play basketball, but I learned more about people. The game taught me independence at the same time I learned teamwork. The game's bottom line is one-on-one, but no one gets to the one-on-one situation without the help of teammates, regardless of skin color. Learning to tolerate various conditions and different people develops character.

At the end of our very good season, Coach McCann called a team meeting. He told us that because of our excellent win-loss record we were invited to the All-Navy tournament. None of us knew much about the tournament except that it was a big honor to be invited! Teams with the best records gathered at Opa-Locka Naval Air Station near Miami, Florida, to compete in a single elimination to determine the Navy's best.

"Do you want to go?" he asked

"You bet we do, coach," said Stan, a black player who was captain of our team.

A bus took us to the Naval Air Station at Glenview, Illinois, where we loaded into a cargo plane. Flat hats were stowed in our handbags. Instead we wore our "watch caps," navy blue stocking hats, and our turtleneck sweaters under standard issue dress blue uniforms and pea coats. We looked like a bunch of shivering penguins, dancing around to keep warm while we waited for the plane's engines to warm up. Knowing the weather in Florida would be much hotter than Illinois, we were ordered to take along a couple of suits of whites. The higher we flew in the unheated plane, the colder it got. The farther south we flew, the more comfortable we became. About half-way through our trip we started peeling off our layered clothes until we were down to our T shirts and trousers. Only when we changed into our white uniforms aboard the plane did we complete what we thought was the transition from Yankee land to the humid, steam-heat of South Florida.

We won our first two games by big scores and began to think, "no problem." Coach McCann told us we could not go ashore until after our last game, but if we won the tournament he would throw a party.

To make a long story short, we lost in the semi-finals to a Marine Corps team from Hawaii. After showers we went with a very subdued coach to the club for a couple of beers that hit us non-drinking athletes hard. Feeling giddy and excited at our first liberty in a new place, the whole team, sans coach, jumped into two cabs and headed for Miami.

The Message of the Puzzle Ring

As we drove along the road toward the city, I stared out the window at run-down shacks and old cars. Opa-Locka was in the sticks, but compared to the North with its bristling commerce and growth, this place looked like a trash heap.

"Can't we make this cab go faster? This is slow -- like watching a worm screw!" a player said.

The team belly laughed and the driver picked up speed.

As we were passing through a small town on the edge of Miami, my buddy Erie shouted, "Stop the cab!"

"Why?"

"There's a bar! Let's get a beer."

The cabs stopped and we piled out.

"Wait for us," Erie told the cabbies. "After we get a drink, we'll zoom on downtown to see Miami."

When we started in the door, a little old lady selling flowers outside the bar said, "Nigger lovers."

I'll never forget her. I had a feeling things were going to go wrong. I looked at Stan. He shrugged his shoulders and kept going. The rest of the team didn't pay any attention either. They just pushed on into the place.

Someone shouted, "Round of beer for everyone, barkeep!"

The bartender seemed irritated but accommodating. After pouring, he slid the glasses along the bar. It reminded me of my first liberty at boot camp.

"Lets have a toast," a guy named Billy Rifles shouted. "To the team!"

Everyone grabbed a glass and held it high. That's when we discovered that our Negro teammates, Erie, Stan, and Suits hadn't been served.

"Hey, what about them?"

"We don't serve niggers here."

"They're our teammates!" I said. "They don't drink, we don't drink!"

"Suit yourselves. Niggers don't drink here."

"Well, screw you!" Rifles said. He turned his glass upside down. So did the rest. We watched as the beer spilled across the bar, then began to walk out.

"Hey, swabs, who's going to pay for this?"

"Here's two bucks," Erie said. "Stick it up your ass!"

"You nigger lovers ain't getting away with this. This ain't Chicago or wherever you came from. You owe me ten bucks!"

"Stick it!"

Two guys from the other end of the bar joined the bartender and the fight was on. I jabbed some fat guy in the eye then got hit with something solid, like a stick. More white civilians got into it before the cops came.

We weren't taken to jail because we were sailors, but we ended up paying the barkeep about $25 bucks.

The old lady was still waiting outside. Wearing a rag for a dress and a snaggled-tooth smile, she said it again, "Nigger lovers."

That evening we whites learned a lot about the human condition in America. We were in Jim Crow's South.

The Team

*****

In the winter of 1950, with the All-Navy Tournament behind us, the team broke up and waited for orders to the fleet. I was released from my duties at the bos'n locker and spent my time hanging around the gym.

Curious about Jim Crow, I made a trip to the base library where I read the laws. Enacted in the southern and border states and enforced since the late 1800's, they mandated colored people to "separate but equal" status. That led to treatment almost always inferior to that provided whites. The most important laws required that public schools, public places, and public transportation, like trains and buses, have separate facilities for whites and blacks.

When my feelings were muddled, I often tried to put myself in the shoes of other people. In this case I couldn't, but I knew Pop Ferger, who was now in his 40th year as a missionary, hated the caste system of India. He must have equally disliked growing up in with Jim Crow, America's caste system. Maybe that was one reason he went to India for his life's work.

My life as a Caucasian seemed very free, and I could not understand anything less. I just thought everyone in the world was living the way they wanted. If they didn't like their circumstances, it was their problem. On the other hand, I had not traveled very far from Pittsburgh.

I was lying on a top bunk in the transit barracks thinking about sea duty and foreign places when I heard the duty petty officer shout my name.

"Yo," I responded.

He said, "Hustle up here, you got a phone call."

Thinking that my mother was the only person who knew how to get in touch with me, I lazily climbed down and walked nonchalantly to the barracks office. I lifted the receiver and said, "Hi, Mom."

"Carl, this is George Frazier."

"George?" What a surprise! How are you?"

We were classmates from kindergarten through high school, but I had not talked to him since graduation. It was the same George I used to fight with when I was a kid.

"Actually very well. You're a hard man to find. Got your phone number from your mom."

"Glad you did. It's been a long time. What's up? Why the call?" I asked.

"Okay. Straight out. How would you like to go to Annapolis? You know, the Naval Academy -- the school in Annapolis, Maryland?"

"Annapolis?" I had heard about the place but never considered it. Frankly I didn't believe I was qualified – my school grades weren't that good.

"Yah. There's a third alternate appointment available from a Pittsburgh congressman. My dad knows him. If you're interested you can have it."

"Why don't *you* take it?"

"I'm happy at Pitt, active in a fraternity, and no interest in the Navy. It's the Air Force for me, but that's a different story."

"I don't have any money."

"You won't need any. If you get in, everything's free."

"Free? Come on, George. What's the catch?"

"Come on yourself. You want the appointment or not?" His voice sounded irritated. "This is a good deal. You can become an officer. You can't lose. I'd jump on it if I were you."

"I'm waiting orders to a ship. I'll finally get to see foreign places."

"Yunz'll get a change of orders – to the prep school."

"Prep school?"

"Yah. Seems the Navy has its own prep school in Newport, Rhode Island."

"I don't know -- let me think." At that moment, Pop's message from Luke 2:52 flashed before my eyes: The puzzle ring, the four-square message: Mind, Body, Social Qualities, Spirit. I heard Pop's voice say, "Aim high."
 I could fulfill my dream of a college education.
 "You nuts? You got to think?" George said. " This is one of the better engineering colleges in America."
 "Okay. Okay. I want it," I spouted. "What do I have to do?"
 "Nothing right now... but pass the entrance exam. My dad will call the congressman's office and they'll take care of anything. You do understand there is a principal appointee and two alternates you'll have to beat out for the appointment."
 "Well. Okay, it's a start."
 "Good man."
 "George."
 "Yah?"
 "Ah ... Thanks for this. How can I repay you?" "Go to Annapolis; become an officer."
 "I'll do my best."
 "Bye and good luck."
 Our conversation lasted less than ten minutes, but it was life changing.
 It wasn't until my 55th high school reunion in 2003 that I could thank George properly. In front of my high school classmates, I told the story about that telephone call and rewarded George, my childhood nemesis turned best friend, by giving him a special gift, an American flag that flew from the main when I commanded the guided missile cruiser U. S. S. Worden CG-18 in Asian Pacific waters.
 Standing in the barracks office with the phone to my ear, I realized that deciding life's work isn't always linear. Sometimes one just takes the first opportunity that comes along, the path of least resistance, and runs with it. As Yogi

Berra once said, "When you come to a fork in the road, take it."

The first thing I did was call my mother.

She already knew about it; she'd given George's father my phone number. "What did you decide?" she asked.

"What would you do?" I asked. "This is another big decision."

"What did you decide?" she repeated.

"I told George 'yes.'"

"Do you still wear Henri's puzzle ring?"

"Most of the time."

"And remember Henri's message?"

"Yes ma'am. Mind, Body, Social Qualities, and Spirit."

"You made a sound decision."

"Ah, Mom. I might have a few days leave on the way to Newport. Thought I'd come home for a visit."

"Oh, that would be nice."

After I hung up I thought about Pop, the man who had touched my life when I was so young. If I got into the Naval Academy and made it through, would my life's work ever permit me to touch other lives as his did?

My change of orders took longer than George predicted, but it gave me time to get off base and enjoy some liberty. Now I didn't have practice or school work to hold me back. Most of my buddies went to Milwaukee where they reported, on return, "The girls are very friendly."

I would not want to mislead you. I wasn't a "goody two-shoes."

I interpreted the "Social Qualities" part of Pop's message in the sense that females were not excluded. Although not a chaser, I quickly learned the company of girls was for me. I won't go into the details of my various romances -- suffice it to say that I found the female of the species just as interested and willing as I was, if not more so.

I became interested in a special girl. I don't remember how we met. I think it was at a dance hall in Milwaukee called the Eagles Club. In any case, to be with her I went on liberty as often as I could. We necked in movie theaters, the back seat of a car, and in the park – anywhere we could be alone.

I didn't know a great deal about the Naval Academy in Annapolis, but the one thing I did learn was midshipmen could not be married. Therefore my goal was to enjoy the Milwaukee girls but to avoid, at all costs, any thoughts of marriage.

On our last date I told her about Annapolis. She seemed to understand and we agreed to write.

My visit to Pittsburgh was long enough to get to know my mother's new husband, a good and decent man with a broad smile and black hair combed straight back. He seemed to care for my mother better than my father ever did. But I was aloof around him – he was different from my father and it was too late for a step-dad relationship.

When loafing around my mother's home became too boring, I had some fun with a few of my high school buddies. Some, like George Frazier and me, I hoped, would struggle through college. Others were contemplating joining the armed forces to fight in a possible war in Korea.

I arrived at the Naval Academy Prep School in March 1950. After all my high school work was reviewed, I began a two month accelerated course of instruction to prepare me to take the entrance exam in early May.

If everything went well, I would enter in the summer of 1950 with the class of 1954; however, I missed entrance by a single fraction of a point in one subject, a 2.4 when a 2.5 was needed. One of the other congressional appointees, if he passed, would enter in my place.

Basketball and Pop's MBSQS again stepped in to become my vehicle of recovery. The coach at the prep school found me in the gym and saw to it that I would stay on for the next season and have another chance at the entrance exam.

Since the new academic year didn't begin until September, I was again left to hang around the base. I spent a lot of time playing basketball, but more time on liberty.

During that summer I had another life-changing event, one that I remain ashamed of, that I still would not want my mom or Pop Ferger to know about.

On arrival back to Newport from one of my liberties, I went straight to my bunk. In less than an hour I had to report for a four-hour stint as barracks fire watch.

In those days I had plenty of energy for liberty but little else. I could fall asleep at the drop of a hat. I crawled into my bunk and my eyes were no sooner closed than I was awakened to relieve a guy named Brzlief, the only sailor at the school permitted to wear a mustache -- some religious thing. I washed my face, brushed my teeth, ran to sign the log, and began what was to be four hours of utter boredom.

My job was to walk the corridors of an empty barracks in a clockwise direction, shining my flashlight up and down. At the end of the first hour I signed the log, "All Secure," and started the second hour walking in a counter-clockwise direction. This time I shined the light left and right. By this time I had been awake for over thirty hours.

The next thing I remember was, "Wake up, sailor!"

I don't remember how I came to be asleep on a pile of mattresses in that empty room, but I do remember the weight of the duty officer's battle lantern on my chest and the light of it glaring in my eyes.

I sat upright and snapped to attention, but it was too late.

"You're on report for sleeping on watch!" the officer said. "You'll be busted and get the brig for this! They'll send you to the fleet!"

The next day I stood outside the office of the commanding officer in my dress blue uniform, waiting to be punished. I didn't know what to expect, but I did know that this kind of offense was very serious. In the old Navy it would have meant a dozen or more lashes with the cat-of-nine tails or even keelhauling, which was even worse.

"On the other hand," I said to myself. "This may be my destiny — no Academy and shipped to the fleet, but that won't be all bad." By now orders to a ship sounded very good.

"What's gonna happen?" I asked the escort petty officer.

"Don't know. But this captain is tough," he added. "When you go in, sound off with your name, rank, and serial number."

I walked to the front of the captain's desk and sounded off.

The commanding officer, a portly man, stood behind a desk. Another officer stood next to me.

Looking at me with unforgiving eyes, the captain asked the stranger, "Sleeping on watch. Anything to say?"

"No, sir. He apparently lay down on some mattresses and fell asleep."

"What do you have to say?" His eyes had a glassy, bored look as if he had heard it all before.

"Nothing, sir."

What else could I say? I did it and I was wrong. I remember thinking of all the excuses I could have made: The watch was as boring as dog shit. There was no need for the watch in an empty barracks, certainly not a continuous watch. That a roving watch by the base fire department would have been enough. And, after all, I was only an apprentice sailor -- the prick didn't have to put me on report. That he could have warned me and sent me back to my post. That I was tired because I stayed out on liberty and hadn't had enough sleep. I found myself thinking about the Bill of Rights, the Articles of the Constitution, and MBSQS. But that would be sniveling.

"I did it, and I'm sorry," I confessed.

"You understand how serious this is?"

"Yes, sir."

"I'm not sure you do." He added, "I'm thinking about notifying your mother of the offense."

That almost floored me. Notify my mother? What for? I'm no little boy. It wouldn't kill her, though maybe figuratively. But it *would* kill me! I'd learned a lot from her: good manners, sensitivity to the feelings of others, hard work. Above all, she wanted me to be a good man, to make something of myself. I had really let her down. I hadn't learned crap from my dad and didn't care if the captain told him. In fact, that would be a *good* thing. It would hurt him to know his son screwed up.

The captain went on. "You want to become an officer, yet you were assigned a watch to protect your shipmates and you let them down. They depend on you to discover a fire, should one break out, alert them and the base fire department thus saving their lives and saving the Navy the cost of a new building. Besides all that, the watch is intended to train you to remain vigilant and take all assignments seriously. Everything we do here is designed to prepare you to become a midshipman and an officer in the United States Navy, assuming you pass the entrance exam."

"Yes, sir." I was in pain with remorse and shame. I deserved the lecture, which went on forever. My mind skipped to Pop Ferger and the message of the puzzle ring. Oh, how I let my friend down.

"This is most serious. Our training is to imbue you with a sense of obligation and duty. Deeds! It's deeds that count -- and you failed miserably. If you were an officer or even a sailor aboard ship, you would be court martialed."

"Yes, sir." My head dropped a bit lower. *Oh, God*, I thought. *Let this be over. Kill me, whatever, but let me suffer in solitude.*

"But here at the prep school, we are going to be lenient and handle it at Captain's Mast."

"Yes, sir." My head dropped even lower.

"Stand up... tall!" he barked. "Chin up!"

I jerked to my full 6'3".

"Anyone want to say something on his behalf before I decide his punishment?"

To my surprise, the strange officer spoke up, "He's got a good record in the Navy so far, sir. Got through boots OK. Played ball for the Great Lakes team that went all the way to the semi-finals of the All-Navy Tournament. Never been in any other trouble."

"Hmm. A ball player. What position?"

"Forward or center, sir." I wondered if all captains liked jocks.

"Anything else? How's he doing in school?"

"Satisfactory. Has a chance to pass the entrance exam. He is working out with the basketball team -- may explain some low grades."

"Working out with the team, is he? Well, that's favorable. Is Navy interested in him?"

"Navy's coach is interested -- knows about him."

"Anything else? No? All right. Let's see. I should send you to the fleet, but -- hmm, basketball. All right, this is an exception. I hereby find you guilty of sleeping on watch. Your punishment is ...?

Kill me. Get it over. But don't tell my mother.

"Still only an apprentice? I can hardly bust you -- you're already as low as you can be. Well, I guess I could bust you back to a one stripe recruit, but, hell, at that rate you'd never make seaman. Let's see. OK, three days in the brig -- bread and water. Dismissed."

Oh, shit. I'll live, but I don't want to. The brig? I never wanted to go to jail and this is a Marine jail! Why didn't he order me killed? I wonder if he'll tell my mother.

"Ah, sir --"

"Yes?"

"You won't tell my mother, will you?"

The captain, who was almost out the door, stopped and stared at me. He waved off the petty officer who was about to pull me a way.

He looked at me and said, "That's a problem for you, isn't it, son."

I nodded.

"All right. This time, but never again. Don't ever come before me again, you hear?"

I nodded. I felt tears well up but I wouldn't let them flow.

That afternoon two petty officers marched me to the brig where I was checked in with a marine sergeant who had me undress, take a shower, and put on prisoner clothing. I was led into a cell. The door slammed shut and I sat down on a cot in the otherwise empty room. My elbows rested on my knees, chin on my chest. In misery I contemplated my future. *I guess I'll be sent to the fleet -- a ship out of Norfolk probably. Deserve it. Never really wanted to become an officer anyway. Bread and water? Never been without food before. Can it be that bad?*

"OK, shitbird. On your feet. You're not here for a holiday, and you're no longer in the fucking Navy. Marines run this brig."

The door slid open and another sergeant stood before me, his chin less than a half inch from mine. "Stand at attention, shitbird!"

Still feeling sorry for myself, I stood, but my shoulders slumped forward. Whining to myself, I said, "My God, what have I done? Screwed up my entire life?"

"I didn't hear you say, 'Yes, sir?"

"Yes, sir."

"Say, 'Sir, yes, sir.'"

"Sir, yes, sir."

"You will say that to every order. Understand?"

"Sir, yes, sir."

"Now, asshole. Shake it off. Stand tall. Understand? In this Marine brig we have pride. Throw your shoulders back! Head up! At attention! Eyes straight ahead! I said head up! Put your hands behind your head. None of that forlorn Navy shit in here. You can feel sorry for yourself after you're back with that sorry outfit. For three days you will feel proud. You're in the Corps, understand? But you'll never be a Marine."

"Sir, yes, sir."

I estimated it was only about 8 o'clock that night when the lights went out and we were told to sleep. The bunk mattress was no more than a half-inch thick resting on a wooden box. I was aware there were other prisoners, but not many. The brig must have been mostly empty because not many voices gave the response, "Sir, yes sir" to the order to go to sleep.

It was still dark outside when the lights went on and a stick rattled across bars. I estimated it was 3:30 or 4 in the morning.

"OK, shitbirds, on your feet! Get in and out of the shower as fast as you can, then put on clean clothes."

"Sir, yes, sir." The sound of multiple voices echoed through the hollow building.

There was no hot water and the brig was so cold we didn't linger in the shower. They wouldn't let us, anyway.

We carried our dirty clothes to a wash area and were ordered to scrub our socks and underwear by hand with soap and a brush, and then hang them on a clothesline.

On return we put on striped prison uniforms stenciled with the big letter 'P.' We were taken to the exercise area and in doing so, passed by the brig mess hall. Until then I hadn't felt hungry, but the smell of ham, eggs, and coffee hit me in the pit of my stomach. Never in my life had I not had a good breakfast. But waiting for me back in my cell, after a half hour of exercise, was a tray with only two pieces of bread and a metal container of water.

"You can have all the bread and water you want," the Sergeant repeated.

We spent the rest of the day doing manual labor, like sweeping the streets and digging holes. I was so embarrassed that I hid my face whenever another sailor from the prep school came near.

How did I feel? How would you feel? In my mind I had fallen down a big pipe and landed in a bucket of shit. Every thought drove me back to Pop Ferger and his challenge. I had failed.

Though prisoners were not allowed to talk to each other, we whispered short sentences and learned each other's names and why each was there. I was surprised. Some were real criminals, rough guys who had raped, stolen, or battered. One guy was in for murder, just waiting to be sent to Leavenworth.

I spent only two days on bread and water because the day of entry was counted as one and I was released early on good behavior on what would have been the third day.

Having completed the most humiliating experience of my life, I had only one thought. It was the loss of my freedom. *I now know why I love going on liberty so much -- the feeling of freedom.* Nothing bothered me more than the feeling of total loss of freedom that jail brings.

But it was also the feeling of hunger. As if I had been in there for a month, the first thing I did after checking back into the prep school was head for the 'gedunk' stand where I bought a milk shake, a soda, two hot dogs, and two candy bars.

I was smoking a cigarette and drinking the coke when my buddy came in and sat down next to me.

"How was it?" he asked quietly.

"Never wanted to go to jail in the first place, and now I know why."

"Rough, huh?" Then he added in a comforting tone, "Never shoud'a put you in the brig – that was an empty building."

"Yah, well I learned a big lesson. Marines, no sleep, bread and water."

"They going to let you stay?"

"Haven't said otherwise. A yeoman told me they probably won't send me to the fleet because I play basketball. No matter how they decide, I know one thing. The brig changed me. From today on I'll be squared away. I'll never let my shipmates down again and I'll never again loose my freedom."

Vijaiji with his Boy Scouts

Chapter 9
Founding the Indian Boy Scouts

Long before the Navy punished me with three days bread and water in a Marine brig, and even longer before I met him at Camp Greenwood in 1943, Henri had learned how difficult it would be to help young men to mix and rise.

Just as skin color kept American men and women separated by Jim Crow laws, Hindu and Muslim boys were tied to a religious and caste belief system that stood in their way. Family or tribal hatreds served as barriers to open minds. Still others just lacked the confidence to live in a changing world -- they quit school early and returned to the farm. Some left to become *chelas* – beggars or disciples.

A major difficulty was the Indian system that gave no opportunity to rise above the caste to which a person was born. Henri, alas, needed a way to overcome the implications of the many cultures. He felt that his boys should offer their friendship to people of all races and nations and to respect them even if their beliefs differed from their own.

The Boy Scouts (see Appendix E) was founded in August 1907, the year Henri entered Princeton. Not long after, British expatriates started the Boy Scout movement in India. But non-Anglo Indian boys were not permitted to become Scouts, nor was it permitted for troops to be organized in Indian schools.

It wasn't until Henri worked at the New Jersey reform school and later at Gordon College that he took an interest in Scouting as a means to assist boys to become men.

On their return to India in 1915, Henri and Kitty became very interested in integrating the Boy Scout program with their educational and religious teachings. They thought Scout values were as important for Christian growth as school and that the Indian caste system was the denial of universal brotherhood. According to the second law, a Scout is a friend and brother to other Scouts. A Scout offers friendship to people of all nations and respects them even if their beliefs and customs are different from his own. Henri believed a Scout could be a brother to every other Scout no matter the social class, race, caste, or religion.

While teaching at Forman Christian College in 1915, Henri tried to start a troop in the local mission school. It was unsuccessful, largely because the boys lived and went to school in one part of the city and Henri lived and worked in another, and he had no other contact with them. Henri's next Scout work in India was to take over a group at the world-famous Woodstock School at Landour, India, in the summer of 1916. These boys were a patchwork of English, American, and Anglo-Indian, largely sons of missionaries. He did that each summer for three years keeping two jumps ahead of the boys as he taught semaphore and knot tying.

Henri wrote, "It was necessary to devise a plan patterned on Scouting <u>but different</u>. It had to accommodate language, religion, and other cultural aspects of the country. I framed an equivalent to the word "Scout" in the Hindu vernacular, but the only possibilities were two words, one meaning 'spy' and the other 'ambassador.' Neither would be satisfactory. I had two meetings with a group of boys trying to carry into practice my plans, but it was not a success.

"My next attempt was better. After teaching two years at Forman, I was transferred to be principal and president of the mission's boys high school at Dehra Dun."

Henri attended his first Scout rally on January 3, 1916, with only British and American children. In November of that first year he attended the first India Scout council followed in December with the Bombay Scout Rally.

Although Mrs. Annie Besant founded the first Scout troop in India for British boys, it was Henri who founded the first Hindu Boy Scout troop in *North* India at the Mission High School with 15 boys in January 1918.

After school closed in early May 1919, Kitty, whose only involvement in Scouting was embroidering second class and merit badges, went directly on to the hills while Henri proceeded on a two week tramp with his Dehra Dun scouts: four Christians, one Muslim, and six Hindus (four of whom were Brahmin (the highest caste). Into the Himalayas they went, carrying their own packs, suffering achy shoulders and tired legs, which they got used to after a few days.

Scouting became Henri's preferred form of evangelism, and he worked ceaselessly (in addition to his job as school principal) on organizational matters at the regional and national levels as well as in the local activities of his own troops.

As stated by John Ferger, Henri's son:

My dad was constantly making trips to distant cities on crowded Indian trains, wearing Indian garb, to attend board and committee meetings at which he was often the only non-Indian present. Closer to home he organized summer camps and endless first-aid competitions. He took groups of boys to help with crowd control, messenger services, and sanitation work at the huge Hindu religious festivals that brought literally millions of people together for days in sacred places.

One problem facing the growth of Scouting in India at his time was that there were no less than five million *sadhus* or holy men who began as *chelas* (in English, a religious student or disciple) and trained boys for that same kind of life. Because Boy Scouts were by and large unknown and little understood, they were often taken for robbers, circus performers, or police. To counter this faulty impression, Henri encouraged his boys to render social services wherever they went.

Henri described his progress in this letter.

Here is some of our beginnings and the history of the past year since the fifteen boys met at my house for the first time. I had something of a vision of what we might do together, but what they have done has far exceeded my dream. I had tried to tell them beforehand something of what it meant to be a Scout, but the chief idea which they had, and I fear some parents, was that it was in some way connected with the war (WWI) and that as soon as their training was completed, they would be sent off to Mesopotamia or East Africa.

We began with fifteen. Only six of those original Scouts, for various reasons, are still with us. But we have grown steadily until at the present time there are, including four officers, a total of forty-nine in the troop. Six are as yet only recruits, having been recently admitted; three have passed only their Tenderfoot examinations; eighteen have done this and have finished more or less of their 2nd Class tests; seventeen are complete 2nd Class Scouts and are now working on their 1st Class tests. One boy has finished his 1st Class tests. I believe he is the first to do so in the whole of North India. Twenty merit badges, in athletics, astronomy, cooking, cycling, and scholarship have been won by ten different Scouts. At the present time a total of 36 are taking the course of six weekly lectures of the St. John's Ambulance Association. This will make it much easier for them to render intelligent aid at times of accident or other emergency.

We have made six trips of a day each to various places about Dehra Dun, several times cooking our own food. Seven of us went on a ten days-trip to Tehri last summer, our first trip of any length. I will not soon forget how thirsty we were as we climbed the Rajah's road from Nagal that hot May morning, or how hungry we were that night, or how tired certain Scouts were the next day when we began to carry our own loads and how their shoulders ached, or how disappointed we were in the sweet rice our head cook cooked for us one day, or how cold we were seven of us trying to all get under one blanket the night that our luggage toques did not come. We are looking forward to a larger and longer trip next May, as soon as the long-hoped-for promotion examinations are over and the holidays begin. Seventeen of us made a three day trip to Rikshikesh and Hardwar last September, perhaps the most enjoyable trip we have had. The most vivid thing I remember about that was the kindness with which we were treated everywhere, at the Kali Kumliwala Dharamshala at Rishikesh, at another Dharamshala at Hardwar founded by the grandfather of one.

Henri's hand in scouting went far beyond his own troops; he helped start troops in several other places.

He wrote in one of his letters.

"In 1921 Sir Robert Baden-Powell came to India and held several camps and rallies to signal the newly-formed mergers of Anglo and Anglo-Indian Scouts, usually of three days each, in half dozen or so places over India. That for the United Provinces was held at Lucknow, with 1200 in

Indian Boy Scouts doing tricks

camp for three days, each troop doing its own cooking. Some 45 Scouts and three officers of our Dehra Dun troop attended. We were almost the only Scouts with more than a few months experience and the only troop with Scouts who had qualified for the King's Scout Badge, the highest award (roughly comparable to the Star Scout Badge of the B.S.A.) Our troop received the honor of being named the First Baden-Powell Troop of the United Provinces (1ˢᵗ B.P., U.P. for short) and received a small silver cup from Baden-Powell himself."

From 1922-1924 Henri and Kitty left India to attend to family matters (see Chapter 16 and Appendix D). On their return, Henri assumed the post of principal of the American Presbyterian Missionary School in Jhansi. From then on the Ferger's life became one of alternating long periods in education and missionary work separated by short furloughs in the USA. Under his leadership in Jhansi, Boy Scouts grew to 18 troops of Hindu, Christian, Muslim, and Parsee boys. (Parsees had migrated to western India from Persia over a 1000 years ago).

Henri remained seven and a half years at Jhansi. After a furlough of a year and a half, he was transferred to another of the high schools for boys at Farrukhabad, U.P., where he remained for two full terms (15 years) until 1949. There he had five or six troops, all of whom learned the three finger salute with their right hand raised to their temple and the Boy Scout pledge:

> On my honor I will do my best
> To do my duty to God and my country
> and to obey the Scout Law;
> To help other people at all times;
> To keep myself physically strong,
> mentally awake, and morally straight.

Henri believed service to be the very center of Scouting. His boys helped individuals and the community in every way they could. His school troop's first experience was at the Tapkeshwar Fair where they wore their new uniforms and bright shoulder knots for the first time, and though they felt painfully self-conscious, Henri said in a letter, "They got their first real vision of the spirit of Scouting. It was a tired and happy bunch of boys that left the *mela* that afternoon for we had been able to be of real service."

As part of the troop's birthday celebration, they decided each Scout would make a special attempt to perform as many Birthday Good Turns as possible during the day. Each boy handed in an account the next morning. Henri read them anonymously; like Henri, a Scout does these without any expectation of reward, and not even praise. Here are a few examples:

The Message of the Puzzle Ring

- "I showed the right way to an old blind woman who was in a dangerous place."
- "I helped my mother cooking the food as it was a very rainy day."
- "In our St. John's Ambulance lecture yesterday, when I saw that a boy had no bandage, I gave mine to him so that he might learn how to bandage."
- "A poor beggar came to our house and he was very hungry. I gave him some food."
- "A man was going in the rain. He was wearing only one Kurtia. I took him under my umbrella."

Henri remained active in Scout work at all levels throughout his years in India. As a result, prior to his retirement from missionary work, Henri was awarded the Silver Elephant badge, equivalent to the Silver Buffalo badge in the USA. Created in 1925, the Silver Buffalo Award is given for distinguished, noteworthy, and extraordinary service to youth. Both are scouting's highest accomplishments.

Midshipman Leaders
Author in Center

Chapter 10
Turning Points

While Pop continued to mail letters that described his missionary teaching and scouting in India, my life in the 1950's became like a bouncing basketball, one crazy dribble after another. Like a bomb in a downward dive, first came sleeping on watch, followed by bread and water in the Marine brig, then fear that the captain would not let me take the exam for the Academy, and finally that he would tell my mother.

When the Navy didn't stop me from taking and passing the entrance exam and the captain didn't tell my mother, I read and re-read Luke 2-52 and Pop's MBSQS message again. It lifted my short-lived feelings of depression.

My appointment to the Naval Academy at Annapolis, jerked me back to normal.

I said to myself, "Maybe I'll live after all!"

But I felt terribly ashamed.

While serving my time, like a criminal, in the Newport, Rhode Island base brig, it came to me that Pop's message may not work for everyone or every situation. In this instance, I just plain screwed up – no excuses. Until then I probably looked like a man but was really a boy thinking narrowly, not broadly -- more about self and in-the-moment` than concerned about others.

What had I learned?

I learned that there are no absolutes for MBSQS. I had to think of it as a foundation to think about and plan. Pop's very short message seemed to give me positive energy and helped me think broadly about my life. I had to visualize ones self as a four-square person and think about the future, make my own choices. What I learned was that my mistakes -- alcohol, liberty, and girls -- were leading me down the same path as my father. I learned to take my Bible with me and when in doubt to refer to Luke 2:52. Of course I learned the balance of MBSQS.

My first life's work (or purpose), that of serving my country in the United States Navy (a good decision) didn't begin when I joined as a sailor but when I entered Annapolis in the summer of 1951.

The fact that it happened at all was an absolute miracle. I thought I'd blown it when I was sent to the brig, but it gave me time to pray and think about Pop's message. In my eyes I'd obviously let him, my mother, and George Frazier down. Though none of them knew it, I was completely aware that I would have to face tests like these in the future, and I had to change by learning from my mistakes.

I was confident I could.

At Annapolis, the college that makes fighting naval heroes, I did change.

I applied MBSQS to my life.

No longer reticent and bashful, I began to rise and become what is known as a "squared away" midshipman.

During plebe year I matured in terms of behavior. I became very serious in my approach to military life, and my sincerity and common sense began to show. Peers and seniors began to grade me very high in 'grease' (aptitude for naval service). At one time I was ranked among the very top in the class of 1955. The military part of plebe year went well -- after all, I had already been through boot camp -- but my academic progress lagged.

I did mature behaviorally, but I barely made it through plebe year academics. I had only about a 2.7 grade point average, finding it difficult to keep all the balls in the air. I could focus on one thing at a time, but the Annapolis way was to pile it on in multiple subjects all graded rigorously. As a slow reader, I barely comprehended the key points of technical material. Again basketball saved me. I made the plebe team and won a numeral. The upper class knew that I struggled with some academics and eased off on hazing (the abusive and humiliating pressure and ridicule given to plebes). They left me alone much of the remainder of year.

It was not until plebe year was over and I was on my first midshipman cruise that I finally set foot on foreign soil. In June and July we sailed across the Atlantic into the Mediterranean Sea, stopped at a French port and a Spanish port, and headed for the west coast of Europe and the British Isles. Places like the Netherlands, Belgium, Paris, England, and Scotland had only been a dream until then. Although the cultures were different from America's, I found the people, just as Pop had, always friendly and kind.

Following the cruise, youngster year came and went quickly. It was during the second-class year, the third year of our training, that I ran into a wall. Things began to distract me. I continued to do well in military subjects and those in which I could apply theory, but I was terrible in left-brain memory stuff, like math and engineering. My main distraction was falling in love.

While I was home on Christmas leave in 1953, a family friend invited me and one of my classmates to her home for a spaghetti dinner. While we were eating, her daughter Barbara flitted through the dining room. I had known her for years but thought of her as a chubby teeny-bopper. I learned that there is love at first sight! She had changed into a beautiful woman.

As soon as I returned to the Academy, I wrote and asked if she would come to Annapolis for a weekend. She agreed. Then I asked her to come for June Week and the Ring Dance, and soon after I asked her to marry me. She said "yes" even though we would have to wait one year until I graduated.

Distractions.

The spring of 1954 brought me to one of the most painful and harsh periods of my life. I failed the final exam for second-class thermodynamics.

Why? No excuses.

How does it feel when you flunk a course? Rotten. Rage! Sick.

Without whining, I can only offer that, at the time, I was love struck and had a hell of a case of flu -- for which, not wanting to take time from cramming, I was doctoring myself, high temperature, snot, and all. I just took a lot of APCs, the Navy's equivalent of aspirin.

Even though I failed the course, I was sent on second-class cruise, where as one of the top-ranking midshipmen in aptitude, I was given a very demanding job. As midshipman navigator on the USS Missouri, I was the boss of all the other midshipmen. On completion of cruise, instead of going on a well-earned leave, like everyone else, I had to stay in Annapolis and retake the thermodynamics exam. Again I failed.

Why? No excuses. It was not unfair; every other classmate had the same chance. I just didn't study properly for it.

The Message of the Puzzle Ring

During that summer of uncertainty, my fiancée drove back and forth from Pittsburgh, spending the weekends at what is called a "drag house," homes in Annapolis where single women stay while visiting Midshipmen.

We talked about leaving the academy for a civilian college, the GI bill, and getting married. But when I seriously considered resigning, I thought again of my secret friend, Pop Ferger, and his four-square MBSQS message. What would he do?

I felt compelled to finish what I started. I really wanted a Navy career. Barbara felt so-so about it, but we decided to stay. She would continue to work another year.

During an interview at a long green-covered table, surrounded by professors, I slumped in embarrassment and humiliation. The superintendent, a tough, crusty old vice admiral, a veteran of Korean War fame, would have none of it. "Sit up! Sit up, mister, tall and straight!" The academic board thought I had potential and offered me what is called "turn back" to the class of 1956. I would have to repeat the entire second-class year curriculum.

Having to repeat an entire year of one's life was the most debilitating things the academy asked of midshipmen at that time. No other college required an additional year of drudgery for failure in one course.

I cruised though second-class year academics like a rabbit chasing a turtle. My grades were so excellent they sent my academic standing at least a third higher than they would have been, even with lack of effort on my part. The best part was that I was transferred to the 10th company with all new classmates.

During my first-class year I was named Midshipman Commander of the 10th Company for both the fall and spring set. Again I was near the top, this time in a new class.

Even though repeating an entire year was a waste, in later years my wife and I felt we had made the right decision.

For us, my naval career provided a more exciting and interesting life than we could ever have dreamed.

Using Pop's self-appraisal, I now graded myself as a much stronger person: my evaluation number was close to 80. Of the puzzle ring's four foundations, I was good in three: Body, Social Qualities, and Spirit, and my Mind began to concentrate on scholarship. It was as if my priorities sharpened.

The day after graduation, "my Barbara" and I began the next test of our life together. After a two-and-a-half-year engagement, we were overdue for marriage, but so were others. Our wedding took place on the rainy Monday morning of June 2, 1956, at the Naval Academy's St. Andrews Chapel. Barbara's extraordinary beauty in her white gown brightened everyone's day.

Wearing my new gold ensign stripes that matched the buttons on my white summer dress uniform, I stood with legs shaking like a wet puppy dog. Next to me was my brother Gordon and pals Van Freeman, Danny Michaels, and Stan Booth. It was a fun wedding with almost everyone in our combined families attending. After a honeymoon in Maine and a short assignment back at the Academy on the commandant's military staff as a company officer for the new plebes, we were off to do our part in the Cold War. I had orders to flight training in Florida, so we headed south.

Soon after arriving in Pensacola, we realized how different it was. We were both accustomed to a big Christmas tree, lots of snow, and a fireplace to cut the chilly air. Instead the weather was hot and muggy. Our apartment barely had space for the tiny imitation tree we bought from a local store. From there we had to listen to *You Ain't Nothing But A Hound* Dog sung by Elvis Presley and played over and over at a nearby drive through restaurant. To keep our sanity, we brought home a dog named Wendy.

Wendy wasn't a particularly beautiful dog. In fact she was a down right ordinary brown mutt with white spots. We picked her from an abandoned litter of "Heinz 57" puppies at the local dog pound. She was friendly, full of life, and "my Barb" fell in love with her.

I knew Barb most of my life. She was never the whiny kind. But as this Christmas approached she became withdrawn. It was just the time of the year and all the things that had happened since June. By nature she was a private person with only a few close friends. As soon as we brought Wendy home she seemed to perk up, finding companionship in the dog, particularly on days when I was in training on the flight line.

About a month before Christmas, Wendy disappeared from the yard. We figured someone thought she was lost and took her home.

As a newlywed husband, I didn't know what to do, not that I would ever be good at diagnosing a woman's off moments. I hugged her and listened, but nothing helped. Wendy was lost, and Barb was pregnant.

Every evening after work I took off my khaki uniform, put on civvies, and set about the task of finding the dog. Driving our 1950 Chevrolet on every street of that small town turned out to be fruitless.

We even bought an ad in the local newspaper and for the next two weekends we waited anxiously by the phone. It never rang.

After weeks of trying everything, Barb buried her face in my chest. "She won't show up. She's lost and she doesn't know how to get home. Poor puppy. I want to go home, No, I don't want to go home. I just want my dog. Where is she? Where's Wendy?"

"I know," I tried to console her as I stroked her hair. "It'll be okay, hun. She'll show up -- wait and see." In truth I really didn't think we would find Wendy.

It must be true, I thought, *that the skin of a woman during pregnancy takes on a special hue.* Barb seemed more beautiful than ever with her brown hair drifting across her shoulders. My hand touched her rounded belly and feelings I never previously experienced tugged at my heart. Machismo learned as a boy and reinforced during Navy training gave way to what I supposed were feminine feelings.

"You must think I'm a wimp," she said. "Crying over a dog."

I kissed her forehead and offered dejectedly. "I'm sorry, honey. I just don't know what else to do. I miss her too."

Barb suddenly stiffened. She stood up and wiped away her tears. "My gosh, what kind of a Navy wife will I be if I let a missing dog get me down? There's still hope! We can still find her and... if not, maybe someone nice has found her."

I've got a lot to learn about women. Just when I've given up, she rebounds.

On my way home from the flight line, a few days before Christmas, I spotted an old two-seater bi-plane parked on an open field next to a dirt road. Curiosity got the better of me. I stopped and walked around the old relic touching the wings and tugging at the rigging. I was about to leave when an older man with a grease-streaked beard eased his head from under the cowling and asked, "You one of those Navy flyers?"

"Not yet, sir. But if I get through the training I will be."

"Well, I watch you fellows day after day -- never had any fancy school training myself -- been fly'n all my life though. Ole Babs here gets me around -- not as fancy as those planes you fellows fly. Course, I don't fly her all the time -- just a few times a year."

"You call your plane Babs? That's funny. My wife's name is Barbara. Some of her friends call her Babs -- I call her 'my Barb.'"

"That so," said the pudgy man, pinching his eyes into a twinkle.

"Yes, sir, but we've got a problem."

"Hmm. Well, some men and women do have problems."

"No, I didn't mean it that way." Then I told the grizzled pilot about Wendy and how her loss was affecting our Christmas.

"Tried to spot her from the air yet? Course not. Well, my contract isn't until later this week. I have to check out the route anyway; come along."

Before I could say no, the old man closed the engine cowling, wiped his greasy hands on a rag, jumped into the back seat, and started the engine.

He motioned me to the front and shouted above the noise and vibration. "Climb in and let's take a look."

The plane bounced down the dirt road and took off skimming just above the tops of cars passing on the nearby highway. I knew the Navy would skin me alive if they ever heard I was flitting around in this rattletrap.

We climbed just above the telegraph poles and searched the city for my Barb's dog. Old Babs weaved across the town buzzing places a dog would go, like where children lived, schools, and drive-in restaurants. Whenever we sighted a white and brown spotted animal we circled, wing tip pointed down, like flying around a pylon. Our heads poked out of the cockpit until I motioned, no, it's not Wendy. Then we would fly on with the old man's white mane blowing with the wind.

After more than an hour he landed the plane.

"Well, son. Tell your Babs that my ole Babs gave it her best shot."

I shook his hand, thanked him, and was about to leave when he said with another twinkle. "Had a similar thing happen to me once -- with my wife -- went out and bought her something new -- like a new hat. It took her mind right off the problem. Maybe you should consider trading in that old 50 Chevy – I don't know – it's just a thought."

I thanked the pilot again and drove off.

In my heart I had lost hope of finding the dog, but after work the next day I did what he suggested. I went searching for a substitute for Wendy -- a new car. I found a used 1955 Chevy with air-conditioning, sporty fender wings, and a new radio.

It wasn't easy to convince Barb to go see it. She thought her 50 was just fine and besides, she was too busy. "I have Christmas presents to wrap and things to do for our first Christmas. Besides, I hope you haven't fallen for the old "buy her a new hat" trick. That's a typical man's trick. I'll still miss that puppy and I won't give up hope."

I gulped and told a white lie, "It's not like that."

I persisted and finally convinced her to come along, to at least take a look.

It was the first time Barb had left the house in several weeks and although she sat passively, I could see her eyes flitting from yard to yard, obviously still looking for Wendy.

"How do you like it?" I asked, pointing to the shiny "55 Chevy.

"Too expensive," she said.

"But do you like it?"

"It's nice, but... "

"It's Christmas, honey. Let's make this "our" present. We need a newer car, one that'll get us back home to Pennsylvania for a visit without trouble." I implied a trip even though I knew my military schedule wouldn't permit it. I was trying everything to divert her thoughts from the Wendy.

Barb seemed to brighten as I showed her the new interior and described how smoothly it would drive.

"Take it for a ride," the salesman said. "But, look -- don't take me wrong, but -- this is Christmas eve -- don't take too long. I've got to get home to my wife and kid."

"You drive, Barb. See how you like it."

"Don't want to."

With the salesman in the back seat we drove around the block and when we returned we agreed to buy it. After signing the last document and writing the check, I offered her the keys again. "You drive."

Again she said, "No. I don't feel like it."

Once out of the lot and on to the main street, I began testing the features of our new car and explaining them to her. I turned on the car radio. *Silent Night* and other Christmas carols filled the airways.

As we drove, her eyes never stopped looking, but I could see they had filled with tears.

I reached to touch her, to comfort her.

"Just leave me alone." She said, wiping her eyes so she could continue to scan the street ahead. Barb and I rode on in silence. Obviously buying the new car was not a substitute for Wendy.

I was still demonstrating the car's new features when we turned onto our street. It was almost dark. I switched on the headlights.

A white spot moved briskly from the shadows into the glow, along a row of hedges. The spot stopped and scratched itself.

"Stop the car," Barbara screamed.

Her face changed. The sadness evaporated and her lips spread into a smile.

I slammed on the brakes and Barb jumped out. She ran to the dog, picked her up, and hugged her.

"It's Wendy. I knew we'd find her," she said holding the dog for me to see. "Poor girl. She's covered with grease, but... Oh... what a wonderful Christmas present!"

As I stood watching my beloved's happiness return, there was an interruption on the radio: "The police are seeking the pilot of an old bi-wing airplane seen buzzing dangerously low over houses."

I heard an aircraft and said to myself, *I know the sound of that engine. Could that be Santa?*

*****

In the spring, I soloed and would have been sent to jet pilot training before I realized that leading men at sea in command of ships had always been my first choice. Barbara was pregnant, so I had to decide. If I stayed until the baby came, I would probably be stuck in a branch of the Navy that wasn't for me. In the spring of 1957 I dropped flight school for a career aboard surface ships.

My new orders sent me to damage control school in Philadelphia. With her doctor's approval, we raced north in time to settle in for the normal birth of our first child, Jennifer, in the small town of Woodbury, New Jersey, near Philadelphia. Shortly thereafter, we were sent to Newport, Rhode Island, sea duty aboard the radar picket destroyer escort USS Gary DER 326 on Cold War duty in the north Atlantic. Next came promotion to chief engineer, though my rank was still only ensign.

We Americans spent much of our lives under the threat of attack by the Soviets. We knew the Russians, who had been our ally during WWII, were gallant fighters having beaten an invading German army with little else than their bare hands. Our Cold War fear was that they would invade America bringing a communist society.

Military men of our time were asked to protect the country and respond to any attack.

Four ships, in stations extending along an arc from Newfoundland to the Azores, had the responsibility to provide early warning of incoming Russian bombers. A similar line of radar extended across the North Pacific.

Time after time, mostly caused by faulty electronics (spooky atmospherics or communications), these ships called the launch of Air Force fighters from the mainland to intercept incoming aircraft. On each occasion, I know of no real Russian bombers that came our way; nevertheless, we patted ourselves on the back as being the worthy front line of America's North Atlantic Radar Defense (NORAD).

Winter picket duty was harsh with temperatures often subzero and very high seas. Many off-watch days were spent strapped, belly down, knees extended to bunk edges. Meals were eaten from sliding trays surrounded by fiddle-boards.

Sometimes hurricanes drove us from our assigned stations. On one of those occasions, with 80-foot waves similar to those portrayed in the movie "Perfect Storm," GARY escaped south in the direction of Bermuda. Because we were near the end of our 30 days on station, our fuel was already low, and the captain expected me as chief engineer to keep him informed of our fuel status. In order to maintain stability, I ordered all empty tanks to be ballasted.

By the time we out-ran the storm, the ship was equidistant from our homeport of Newport and Bermuda.

After some hand-wringing, the captain made the difficult decision to head home instead of refueling and taking a liberty in that lovely island country.

As we approached the safe waters of Newport harbor, I, the lowly ensign chief engineer, dumped the saltwater ballast hoping to salvage the top few inches of diesel fuel.

We were so low on fuel that to enter the harbor we had to constantly run our centrifuges to separate the residual salt water from the remaining oil. Success was based on the engineers having enough diesel for the ship to make it on its own to a berth alongside the pier without calling for a tug.

With each shot of saltwater, one engine after another shut down. The ship was dead in the water in Newport harbor. Our engineering petty officers ran around cleaning injectors, doing their best to restart.

Finally we gave the skipper enough diesel fuel to creep alongside with one engine.

He conned the ship toward the dock, topside sailors standing smartly at attention in their dress uniforms, and said, "Now don't embarrass the ship. I'm counting on you to not let that engine go dead in this approach."

In true Navy style, and as if nothing unusual had happened on that trip, Captain Childress slipped the proud USS Gary alongside.

The engineers in their sweaty dungarees knew the truth.

Not long after that episode, I received orders assigning me to a brand-new ship, this time as weapons officer.

Things began to move very quickly. USS Decatur DD 936 sailed for the Mediterranean Sea, and now we had two baby girls. We were at the end of our four-year obligated naval service and had to decide whether to stay in the Navy or return to civilian life. A couple of businessmen took me to lunch and invited me to take over their toy manufacturing plant. But Decatur's captain countered with an offer of orders back to the Naval Academy as a company officer, the dean and mentor of about 150 midshipmen. I still loved the Academy, so it was I who convinced Barbara to stay with the Navy at least for a two-year shore duty tour. We told each other that we would reassess sometime later whether or not the Navy would continue to be our life's work.

Looking back at this turning point, it's ironic that Pop Ferger and Kitty made their major life-change to leave their mission and retire at essentially the same time we were caught up in the details of our own lives

In the summer of 1960, my first year as a company officer, I silently worked to introduce Pop's MBSQS resulting in the midshipmen of Company Eleven coming in second place among 24 companies for the coveted Color (best) Company. The next year "Club 11" won the Colors. That led the commandant in 1962, to offer me orders to be the sole naval officer in the military department at the U. S. Military Academy at West Point, New York. Since the birth of our third child, Monica, came on the March 30, 1962, we were free to move on to a new and exciting assignment. As tactical officer in charge of a company of brand new cadets, I soon learned about combat boots, long marches, and bivouacking under tents in open fields. I looked more like a sad sack than any new soldier, yet before I left West Point, my cadet company, F-2, had been introduced to MBSQS resulting in a ranking of best in the Corps. Just like at Annapolis, they had won the Colors.

At the end of my tour at the Point, I watched with pride as the class of 1963 marched to their graduation. I had become quite attached to them and knew that very soon they would go on to great sacrifice fighting our new war in South Vietnam.

By now I had been three years on shore duty with some of the finest officers and men in the Army and Navy. Using Pop's self-appraisal process, I assessed my personal growth at a much higher level than ever before and attributed my improved development to my secret pal, Reverent Henri Rabb "Pop" Ferger, who as far as I knew was still in India.

I knew then that I was ready for command of a Navy ship.

Going Home

Chapter 11
Good Bye, India

In the spring and early summer of 1960, I was a junior naval officer aboard the destroyer USS Decatur on Cold War duty in the Mediterranean Sea. That duty with the Atlantic fleet was soon followed up by our first shore duty. During that time my letters from Pop became sparse. I didn't know then that Henri and Kitty were ending their Christian missionary service in India.

Their years as missionaries and educators overlaid India's most significant change in modern times. Serving from 1910 through 1959-60, they observed first-hand the plight of the people as they struggled through their maelstrom of discontent. It was the nation's greatest period of turmoil including: part of the colonization period of the British Raj, which eventually retreated from India in 1947; World War I; World War II; the non-violent fight for independence; the mass killings during the partitioning; then finally the birth of twin nations, India and Pakistan. (See discussion in Appendix D that explains more fully the term "Birth of Twin Nations").

*****

Even during my days as a student at the Naval Academy, I remained on Henri's list to receive his periodic letters. Although I seldom responded, I read each with interest and remained fascinated with the happenings in India. I wanted to inhabit his world, to know more about the country he served. I read everything about the place.

At the time, I couldn't easily appreciate the history of India. There was too much to absorb, and I was very busy with my own life's work, the Navy. Over time, the story of Henri's service to that nation became clear to me. For an in-depth story, see Appendix C, *India in Henri and Kitty's Time*.

Henri and Kitty clung loyally to their adopted nation, serving year after year through all the changes. But every story has an ending.

Ten years before retirement from their mission to India, Henri accomplished his major personal goal, that of working himself out of a job. He turned over his duties as principal of the Fatehgarth school to Headmaster Mr. James M.G. Ram and moved on to do full-time what previously had been his hobby: audio-visual work under the National Christian Council. Having attended classes at the New York Institute of Photography during several furloughs, he had become an expert in this new field, capturing Christian life in underdeveloped nations. Henri did remain a member of the U. P. State Council of the Bharst Scouts and Guides. (A collection of his excellent photography is held at the Division of Rare & Manuscript Collections, Carl A. Kroch Library, Cornell University.)

In October 1959 the final day came and their work as missionaries was over. They had observed first hand the many changes to the nation they loved as their own. Henri had served India close to 50 years, Kitty 44. They were 70 and 72 years old respectively.

As Kitty described it, the day was burning hot with dust churning in the crowded streets. The mission compound in Allahabad, where the church was located, sat away from the main roads, allowing some room to breathe.

Ageing cream-colored bungalows, their arched verandas burdened with vines, were surrounded by a geometry of flower gardens and thick trees. Early missionaries must have found or built in the only eucalyptus grove in the region. It was a place of great calm.

"Kittydear, do you know what tomorrow is?" Hearing no response to his question, he answered himself. "Tomorrow is an historical occasion."

"How's that, Henri?"

"I mean besides our leaving," He added to his earlier sentence.

"How's that, Henri?" Looking up momentarily from her knitting.

"Well, Kittydear." He raised his voice. "By my calculations, the missionary era in the Punjab has spanned 125 years today. The first missionary came for evangelistic work in October 1834, and today, 1959, equals 125 years!"

"Well, praise the Lord," she said. "That means our church has finally grown up."

Henri knew it was a fading era. During their time in India, they witnessed the dwindling of evangelistic missionaries in the north of India. He and Kitty were among the last of their kind and would be among those closing the era. Not that they were personally unhappy about it – after all, it was their time to leave. But they had seen their colleagues, good ones, retired early and shipped off to bureaucratic roles.

Henri approved the principle of shifting the leadership of the church to indigenous hands but not if that meant shoving out all the church-related missionaries.

For years, letters home were full of passionate appeals to send more missionaries to "reap the mighty harvest." The crop at that time was almost entirely composed of the lowest untouchable caste, the sweepers, who came unsolicited by the tens of thousands to receive baptism and the benefits of getting out of the Hindu caste system.

Henri was known to exclaim, "There's no caste or class in our schools."

But now the cities had many high schools run by the government and some privately by Hindus and Sikhs. The new government schools, built on a vast scale after independence in 1948, were governed by policies that wiped out missionary efforts. Church schools switched to being high schools and technical schools, consolidating their old institutions into a few major centers. At the high school and college level, the Christian institutions had to compete with the large networks of Hindu and Sikh schools. Paradoxically, these were begun earlier in the twentieth century in response to the Christian emphasis on conversion that seemed to challenge Indian religions. Many of the Christian school students had rich Hindu and Sikh tuition-paying parents, thus supplementing the money from America that kept the schools solvent.

No one knew exactly how many village Christians there were. At one time they were estimated at around 500,000, but the latest census gave the figure as 162,000. Christian doctrine had never been particularly well-learned in the villages, and many Hindus didn't bother to keep the westernized or biblical names given them when they converted.

The erosion of Christian membership continued not only for lack of nurture from the church but also because the jobs which the government reserved for "scheduled castes" were not open to those who claimed to be adherents of a non-Hindu religion, and therefore no longer in any caste at all, scheduled or otherwise. Henri fixed the blame for this policy on the church leadership at the time the government, before independence, was drawing up the list of scheduled castes. That leadership was composed of a missionary-trained elite and a few converts from high-caste Muslim and Maharahas families. This gave them some status with the British government, and because of that, they refused to allow Christianity to be placed on the list.

The thing that intrigued both Henri and Kitty was that so many still hung on to their Christian identities despite the obvious liabilities. This was remarkable in light of the fact that those joining the faith in mass movements had but the vaguest notion of what they were getting into. They just knew it was likely to be better than being an untouchable. The converts often renamed their caste "Christian."

Given their economic situation and the sense of estrangement from the old society that belonging to a new faith brings, it was natural that some political movements emerged to protect the Christians' rights and promote their welfare.

They persisted in running candidates in elections they didn't have the slightest prayer of winning because it publicized their demands, such as land for poor landless, protection against anti-Christian and anti-missionary legislation, and protection against occupation of church land. Mostly they wanted the same rights and benefits the scheduled castes were getting. The biggest problem was organization. The poor people didn't have the money, and the rich couldn't be bothered.

Educated Christians, if they passed the state examinations, got government jobs; however, the law prohibiting government employees from being involved in politics might also have been a way of co-opting the scarce leadership of the poor.

Henri framed some questions regarding the sociopolitical character of lower-class Christianity: Was it a movement of the oppressed, or a movement of the oppressors? Was it an escape from reality or a shift to a more authentic alternative society? Was Christianity perceived as the ideology of the foreigner or as the vision of an India fulfilled, its deep divisions made whole?

Another question surfaced that seemed more compelling and immediate. Would Christianity survive at all, given the formidable pressures to assimilate into the dominant culture, and given the absence now of foreign rewards? Henri felt that the question would resolve itself positively, despite the perils, the tensions, and the fears. The Christian community had become a fact on the landscape of India. It had an identity, a culture, an internal world of its own, as secure in India's future as the Muslim community had become after the departure of the Moghuls some centuries before. (Credit is given to Mark Juergensmeyer for his work about the fading era. See Appendix A.)

"Well, Kittydear, it's almost time to go."

Kitty was reluctant. The afternoon rain had come and gone. The ground was already dry. This last house was more to her liking than their earlier dwellings. Originally built for a missionary, it had been converted to a modern ranch-style home, full of bookshelves, with a convenient kitchen made for an American wife rather than Indian servants. The books they inherited included light novels, theology, and school administration.

Slowly their missionary friends, students, and Indian parishioners gathered. Many of the boys had been Scouts in the original troop.

Henri welcomed them and read some Bible passages, gave a long prayer, and made a little speech, illuminating the significance of October 1834, the beginning of evangelism in India.

He recited a list of some of the more illustrious foreign missionaries: John Lowrie and William Reed, Charles Forman, who founded the distinguished college which bears his name; Hervey Griswold, the missionary scholar who pioneered sociology in Punjab; some of the more recent missionary heroes, such as Ernie Campbell, who received an Indian government citation for helping resettle refugees; and William Wanless, M.D., who built a hospital. His list was long but, humbly, did not include the Fergers.

Each of their guests, in turn, stood up and gave short testimonies about the Fergers and their work.

When Henri stood again, he told the gathering with quiet emotion that he and Kitty would miss them and their years of service in this place. "Of course we love India and its people. We consider it our second home. The people are pleasant and the government friendly. God bless India."

Garlands of garish red and gold foil were put about the Fergers' necks in the Indian tradition. Then came the tea, lots of munchy Indian snacks, and pastry with chocolate icing.

At the time to catch the Frontier Mail train, the party moved outside. They shook hands all around, photos were taken, and the group waved as they walked away.

Having lived during the expanse of the political scene and the many incredible changes, the Fergers left behind India's discontent and sailed back to America.

They were ready to enjoy retirement at a home near their son and his family in Dryden, New York, not far from West Point where I was stationed in 1962-63. But neither pal knew the other was so close.

U. S. S. Cocopa ATF 101

Chapter 12
Vietnam, the War

In 1963 when the Navy honored me with orders to take command of my first ship, I was serving on the faculty at the U. S. Military Academy. The Fergers had returned to their homeland at the same time I was moving my family west to take command of U.S.S. Cocopa (ATF 101), home-ported in San Diego, California, a place we knew little about.

Named after an Indian tribe in Arizona, this fleet tug served as an open-ocean towing ship with salvage capability. Our family, now including three beautiful daughters, one of whom was barely a year old, motored across America on Route 66 in the heat of the summer desert. Without modern air-conditioning, all of us were convinced that we had made a mistake moving west to California. As we passed through Balboa Park, where the trees were green and we could see the harbor, we changed our minds. San Diego, considered the land of 70-degree weather, instantaneously became our permanent home.

Sometime after settling my family and taking command of Cocopa, I was asked about taking command of an ocean-going ship when I had so little experience. I had only two ship tours and I had never served as executive officer. Wasn't I nervous?

In truth, at first I was a wreck, but I didn't want anyone to know. My solution was to secretly race to the nearest base library and read everything in print about handling single screw ships, including *Knight's Modern Seamanship*. Although I had made quite a few landings, they had all been twin screws and under the gaze of the captain. Again under the secrecy of home study and the library, I reviewed *Duttons Navigation and Nautical Astronomy*. Shortly after, we (the crew and I) deployed her to the Western Pacific.

I was ready. Just in case, I kept my Bible nearby. It had Pop's note written with the symbol of a square ☐ under Luke 2:52, and I said a lot of prayers. This would be my first transit as commanding officer across a major body of water. October 1963 brought a short stop at Midway Island to watch the Gooney birds (albatross) do their flip-flop landings; we pushed on to Guam.

It was there that we learned of the assassination of President John F. Kennedy. I went immediately to the passage in Luke 2:52 and Pop's MBSQS and prayed. This was a leadership situation for me. I called for my executive officer to round up as many of our small crew who wished to join us at the nearest church, a Catholic cathedral in downtown Agana. There we prayed that God receive his soul and take care of Mrs. Kennedy. On return to the ship, I penned a cable to Mrs. Jacqueline Kennedy that said, "The officers and men of U.S.S. Cocopa (ATF 101) extend our deepest sympathy and share in your grief for the loss of President Kennedy." Not long after, Mrs. Kennedy sent our crew a personal thank-you note.

Serving as commanding officer of Cocopa was by far one of the best jobs of my career, not only because it was my first command, but also because we were one of the earliest U.S. Navy ships to enter the Vietnam war zone.

The Message of the Puzzle Ring

As a young lieutenant assigned to my first ship command, I had a lot to learn. I had spent several years among the spit and polish of Annapolis and West Point, but my measure of Navy worth was command at sea, not a fleet staff job nor a desk in Washington. Now I had this chance.

The early months had been a struggle to tighten up and turn around what, compared to the yards of Annapolis and West Point, was a sloppy ship. The exec, who had more than 20 years in the navy, tried to explain to his new C.O. that the "Tug Navy" was different than Annapolis or even the "Cruiser Navy," for that matter.

One evening I stood on the bridge, gazed across the harbor, and reflected on the previous week. It had ended in disaster. The Friday inspection went so badly I had demanded another field day and a re-inspection on Saturday morning. I remembered the hard looks from the crew as I marched through the ship demonstrating the white glove cleanliness I had learned ashore. I finished my topside liberty and went below for the night, wishing I better understood what made a tug sailor tick.

I was barely asleep when I heard, "Captain!"

The call came a second time. "Captain, wake up!"

I struggled with my thoughts, hoping it was a nightmare or a mistake, because it surely wasn't time to go back to work.

"Cap'n. Wake up, captain. We just got a hot message."

"Um, take it easy," I said shielding my eyes from the blinding rays of the radioman's light. Through a squint I noticed, standing in the background, the exec wearing only khaki trousers and a skivvy shirt. It was 0100 Sunday morning.

My eyes slowly became accustomed to the lights and when the fuzzy words on the paper became readable, they revealed the strangest ship movement orders I had ever seen. The message simply said, "Get under way immediately and head west. Further orders to follow."

"What do you think it means?" I asked the exec.

"Beats the hell outame, skipper," came the response accompanied by a you-got-me shrug.

I bristled inwardly at the casual use of the word "skipper." Captain was the proper term to use in the presence of a commanding officer. If the radioman hadn't been present, I might have given the exec a word of caution. Instead I asked, "Do you think they mean to get underway right now? It's after midnight Saturday!"

"Crap, Skipper. If we're still here in the morning we'll all be standing at attention in front of the admiral, with a pucker where the moon don't shine."

"How soon can we get ready?"

"Lemmesee. Gotta get the engineering plant revved up, and the crew back from Olongapo. Most of' 'em 'll be drunk -- went ashore in a foul mood after your inspection," he said with a biting tongue. "Maybe two hours. May have to go without a few of the crew. Some of the kids may not come back if they're pissed off."

I flinched when the exec mentioned the inspection but passed it off and told him to go to it, even though I, the young skipper, knew two hours was ambitious.

It was 0130 when I wandered back on the bridge. As I waited in the shadow of the pilot house, watching for the crew to come aboard, I felt the deck vibrate and heard the rumble of diesel engines come to life.

The exec had sent a chief to the crew's favorite watering hole. They were mostly eighteen-and-nineteen-year-old bachelors and their home away from home was the Texas Bar. Before long, down the pier they came, staggering one by one, or occasionally with a buddy. Drunk as they were, each straightened up, squared his white hat and adjusted his neckerchief before flashing what I considered a sloppy salute to the OOD. Each slipped casually across the gangway and below to change into working clothes.

The Message of the Puzzle Ring

By 0230, only an hour and a half after he had been awakened with the message, the exec made his report: "The chief couldn't find Fargo, Manning, and Estevarria, but otherwise the ship is manned and ready at sea detail, ready to get underway, skipper."

There was excitement in the air. Orders were relayed efficiently in low, quiet tones. All lines came aboard and I backed her clear of the ship astern. She maneuvered silently from her nest among still-sleeping gray hulls. Green and red side lights and the topside whites were the only things seen moving through the still, black harbor by the mid-watches of the otherwise-resting fleet. She passed Grande Island and swung a long turn for the open sea. Outside the harbor rumors began to spread. One story had the ship on the way to Vietnam. The war there was heating up. Another was they needed a tug to tow targets for a big fleet gunnery exercise. The best was that a merchant ship was aground and we were to pull her off before the next typhoon came to the South China Sea.

Our ocean-going tug steamed at full speed all morning and well into the afternoon. I read and reread the message just to assure myself I had done what I was told. The words on the paper hadn't changed. I was beginning to understand what Columbus must have felt when he received orders from Queen Isabella to sail west and discover the new world.

By late afternoon the bridge watch was whispering and glancing about.

"Ya think we'll get back to Olongopo for Christmas, Cap'n? I told my honey I'd take her to Manila," asked the bos'n of the watch, a petty officer from Pennsylvania who wore his white hat with a jaunty look. It was his way of reminding the skipper that families and girlfriends were coming to join the ship for holidays.

The chief bos'n asked, "When you go'n to tell us where we're headed, skipper?"

The crew suspected that I had a secret and was going to break the news after some significant event in their day, like evening meal. Of course I couldn't, but the bos'n was harder to convince than the judge at the Caine Mutiny court martial.

"It's okay, skipper, so long as we get back to Subic for the holidays." Then the bos'n bragged so everyone on the bridge could hear, "We sure got a get-up-and-go-ship, don't we, skipper? Can you imagine one of those fancy cruisers or carriers or even a destroyer get'n underway on short notice like we did? We're tug sailors!"

The ship was almost 200 miles from Subic, sailing along at a crisp 13 knots when the next message arrived. It read simply, "Proceed to Ream, Cambodia. Lay out of sight of land until diplomatic clearance is granted."

"Where in the x?!!x is Ream?" said the exec, who was also the navigator.

Large charts were spread across the quartermaster's work-table while they searched the coast of Southeast Asia for a place called Ream. They found the Parrot's Beak, Phnom Penh, Sihonakville, and finally a speck called Ream. The ship's only chart of the port, in French, dated ten years before, showed Ream as a small, well-protected harbor with only one shallow entrance.

Several days later the little tug arrived at a point about 25 miles off Ream. Just out of sight of land is not a point where a ship drops anchor to wait. It's a distance outside of which it is expected the ship's masts can't be seen from the highest point ashore. Our tug sailed back and forth for two hot days waiting for the next message.

"Diplomatic clearance granted. Enter Ream, Cambodia, and take possession of U.S. patrol vessel anchored there."

Our approach to the harbor was cautious because one of the seamen, who had studied French in high school, warned that the chart spoke of currents in dangerous terms. The old French chart showed the depth of water in the little channel to be between five and six meters. The tug drew 16 feet of water, but its fathometer was broken, so I had the chief bos'n put a man in the chains with a lead line to take soundings as the tug crept through the narrow channel. I relaxed when I heard, "By the deep four."

The harbor was a beautiful lagoon surrounded by barren coral. In the center of this idyllic anchorage was a modern Patrol Boat (PGM) flying a big American flag.

It is one thing to have diplomatic permission to be in another country's waters, but slipping in to take possession of a boat was a different matter. Ordinarily, the notion that the Cambodian Navy might disagree would incite no more than a sneer from an American naval ship. But our little tug was armed with only one 3" single fire gun mounted on the fo'c'sle, little better than the guns John Paul Jones had when he fought the British.

Not long after the PGM was taken in custody, a tough-looking bos'n mate and a civilian came alongside in a small boat. The sailor had a .45 caliber pistol strapped to his waist, was wearing a black beret, and was dressed in fatigues. The two had driven from the capital to meet us. They were among the last advisors in Cambodia since Prince Sihanok declared his independence from the United States. The American response was to take back any military equipment that had not previously been turned over, and get all military advisors out of the country. The Bos'n said he didn't know how the Cambodian Navy would react. They really admired the craft and because it was in their waters, they had demanded that it be turned over to them. The civilian told us the ambassador thought it best to move her out of the harbor as quickly as possible.

Not long after the two advisors left, the bridge lookout warned that a warship was approaching from seaward. A small coastal frigate soon rounded the coral and entered the lagoon. It was a Cambodian warship returning from patrol. Upon spying the American ship she went to general quarters. Sailors could be seen scurrying about, donning combat helmets and life jackets, just as American advisors had taught them to do. They manned their guns but never pointed them at us. They gave no honors, and none was given by the tug, but several of the American crew stood casually by the single 3" gun with ammunition at the ready, just in case there was a problem.

During the night the Cambodian ship got underway again. Still the young inexperienced skipper, I passed it off. After all, it was their harbor and their water.

Early the next morning, with the PGM at short stay, Cocopa was on the move. As we approached the entrance, the lookout reported that the Cambodian ship was waiting just outside the harbor entrance.

"They could be waiting to give us some special naval honor or they could try to blow us out of the water and take the boat. Don't take no chance, skipper," the exec cautioned.

By now I had learned to listened to my exec. I sent our tug crew to General Quarters.

The Cambodian ship was at full battle stations. All guns were manned, but no gun barrel was trained on us. Our tug approached the destroyer watching for signs of further hostility. Instead, as the Americans passed by, the entire Cambodian crew was brought to attention, but again no honors were exchanged. Instead, in a breach of naval manners, the entire crew of the Cambodian ship did an about face.

Several of our crew raised their middle fingers in return.

Though the Cambodian ship didn't follow the tug, I didn't take a chance. I ordered full speed until well into international waters.

The bridge watch was delirious when they learned the tug could make it back to Subic for Christmas with time to spare. The wheel watch bragged, "I guess we showed them, didn't we skipper? Damn good thing those Cambod's didn't try anything. We'da blown them out'a the frigg'n water. Hell,

The Message of the Puzzle Ring

we do the jobs the spit and polish boys can't do. Subic Bay, here we come."

I winced at the words 'spit and polish.'

It was four days before Christmas when our tug with a stern tow entered the South China Sea. The transit around the Parrot's Beak was uneventful, but the winds were coming from the quarter and wispy clouds were forming. Later that day the seas began to build and a gale had formed. Before nightfall I realized we were in a full-fledged typhoon. There was little to do but button up, slow to steerageway, and hope for the best.

It was late when the stern lookout reported sighting a light aboard the PGM. The chief bos'n reported that the flooding alarm lights were rigged topside and it was important that we get aboard quickly. "She may be sinking!"

By this time the wind was thundering across the water and mountainous waves were breaking over Cocopa's bow.

I assumed it was too dangerous to put men aboard, but the exec and the chief bos'n argued otherwise. "If she floods, we'll have to cut the tow wire and let her go, or she could sink us. We've got to get aboard and stop the flooding, skipper.".

"Are you crazy?" I asked. "I won't order the men and no one would volunteer to go aboard in this kind of storm."

"It's been done before, skipper. Hell, I'll go to make sure it's done right." The bos'n said casually.

"I'll go too," added the bos'n of the watch, the one from Pennsylvania.

"Me too," said three deck seamen in unison.

I gave them my permission and warned them it could be very dangerous. The bos'n disappeared below and soon reappeared on the fantail. A rubber life raft was inflated, and when all was ready, I granted them permission to put it in the water. The shadows of three occupants rose and fell with the heavy seas as members of the fantail crew carefully played out a line attached to the raft. Waves crashed over the men as they paddled toward the PGM. In the fading light, after what seemed an eternity, the raft was alongside.

The PGM had a high freeboard and the men aboard the life raft had to unlash themselves to climb aboard. At that point they stood the risk of being washed away. Cocopa was now in irons and it would have been impossible to maneuver for a rescue.

The raft rose in the water and crashed into the PGM. I could see hands reach for a tight hold just as the next wave tossed the two boats apart. Slowly they came together again and the raft rose high. Again they were washed apart as green water boiled between the two. I was about to call the whole thing off when a mountain of frothing water rose again and hands finally grasped the PGM's rail. One courageous body scampered aboard, then another and another. Finally the raft was aboard and secured on deck. The men became no more than specks in the blackening night. Then they disappeared.

Over the walkie-talkie came the chief bos'n's voice, "Found the problem, skipper."

By now that word skipper sounded like Brahms to me.

"Water's coming aboard through the stern tube. The engineer's making repairs, but it's doubtful it'll last long in these seas. We better get to a port quickly."

The bos'n and his team were ordered back and soon the three appeared on deck. One by one they slipped over the side into the bobbing raft where they hung tight as the fantail crew winched them back to the tug.

Not knowing what to do, I sent a message explaining the danger to the PGM and asked for instructions. I added that Vietnam was the nearest port. Soon the answer was received, "Divert to Saigon. Turn over craft to Military Assistance Command."

It made sense. The ship was three days out of the Philippines and only one day out of Vung Tau and the mouth of the Long Tau Channel to Saigon.

The navigator laid out the course and the little tug, with its tethered ward, crept through the rains, wind, and heavy seas to the west.

The crew sensed the next adventure with nervous excitement and some apprehension. They had heard that Vietcong were shooting up the country.

"Do you think we'll make it to Subic for Christmas, captain?"

"Doesn't look too good. Can't make enough speed. How about Christmas in Saigon?"

On 23 December the little tug struggled into Vung Tau, the Riviera of South Vietnam, where the patrol boat was brought to short stay. A pilot was to guide the tug up the Long Tau Channel on the afternoon flood.

There was just enough time to pump the patrol boat's bilges and check temporary repairs before the transit.

The pilot, a withered old Asian who spoke Vietnamese, French, and Pigeon English joined me for the usual amenities and a cup of the tug's best green tea. When all was ready the pilot ordered, "Slow ahead." But the ship didn't move. When the pilot questioned if the engineering plant was in need of repairs, I became irritated, took the con, and ordered, "Ahead two thirds." When we still didn't move, I ordered, "Full ahead." Still nothing happened except a report from the fantail that the tow-line was under heavy strain and was tending straight down.

The exec reported. "We're in irons, skipper. Hung up on the bottom."

The pilot reminded us that if we missed the tide, the next high was not until morning.

Our divers found that the tow wire had caught the fluke of a half-buried anchor. The depth was near maximum limits for the tug's equipment and the qualifications of their divers. It would be dangerous work. They could work only for short periods, and to make it all more dangerous, the ship would have to be carefully maneuvered from time to time while they worked below to untangle the heavy stiff wire.

I asked, "Should we ask Saigon for help?"

By now the response should have been obvious to me. They had already proved they were good, even if the skipper didn't think they were spit and polish.

"Shoot, skipper, this'll be a piece-of-cake, it's what we get paid to do." With that, every qualified diver on board stepped forward and volunteered.

Air tanks were laid out on the fantail and the dive organized. They swam below in teams of two. In the few minutes each was below, they struggled to back the half hitch over the fluke. After several attempts, word came to back the ship slowly, just enough to give the right amount of slack to the men below.

"Back one-third," was the order from me, and the screw gently turned. It was a carefully coordinated effort with several starts and stops, but after a time a head bobbed from the water with a shout, "She's free."

The next morning the tug was underway for the trip to Saigon. Vietcong were active in the Rung Sat, which surrounded the Long Tau, the only deep-water channel to Saigon. The pilot warned me to expect an attack by guerrillas anytime. So, although it was a scorching day, the tug crew, with more than a few bellyaches, donned battle dress, heavy helmets, and life jackets. On the other hand, it was the first time any of them had been in a combat zone. Hot or not, it was a small price to pay to stay alive.

Five hours, and without attack, the outskirts of Saigon began to take form. The city was teeming with millions of wretched people living in tin and cardboard shacks,It was Christmas Eve when the tug moored at a pier near the center of the city. After members of the Military Assistance Command arranged to have the patrol boat towed away to a safe place, the crew was ready to get ashore for some exotic liberty. But we learned from the boarding party that a general named Big Mihn had just killed the emperor, a man named Bau Dai, and the city was under strict martial law. "Sorry, no one ashore, and the ship will have to leave tomorrow afternoon, on Christmas day."

The crew was disappointed, but with the true genius of tug sailors they responded. "If we can't get ashore, why not bring the fun to us. Let's give a Christmas party."

"How about a party for kids," Howser, a sailor from Detroit said.

Espinosa, the one from Florida said, "Ya, and invite some pretty girls."

Several orphanages were invited to a party in the crew's mess the next day. If a few older females showed up, that would also be okay. The energy and resourcefulness of the tug crew had become less and less a mystery to me. Where does one find a Christmas tree in South Vietnam in less than 24 hours? If the answer doesn't jump right at you, don't feel bad. By noon the next day there it was, a fully decorated tree standing near the galley. Of course the meal was fit for a king, turkey, ham, mincemeat pie -- the works.

The kids who came aboard had Catholic nun manners -- quiet and respectful, with big smiles. They held hands as they stood in a long line leading from the pier to the mess hall. Once inside they took their places and waited patiently as the sailors delivered, with fatherly care, a tray of food for each. The crew forgot only one thing -- chop sticks. The children had never used knives and forks.

The chief engineer played Santa Claus. He sallied forth among the kids in a red suit and a white beard. At first the children were shy, but after encouragement by the nuns, each came to sit on his lap where they were presented a gift. No one could tell who had the most fun at the party, kids or crew.

Like all good things, the Christmas party came to an end. The nuns thanked the crew for the party as the children clung to chambray-shirted tug sailors escorting new little friends off the vessel.

The next day we sailed back to the South China Sea through the crooked Long Tau Channel and the Rung Sat Special Zone, two places that would later become a major part of my life.

Spit and polish had vanished from its lofty position on my list of priorities. I had witnessed dedicated fleet tug sailors do their jobs. Reality is the courage, ingenuity, and compassion of an American bluejacket rising to a challenge.

On return from that cruise, I received orders as executive officer of U. S. S. Morton (DD (948), the same class of ship as my earlier assignment to U.S.S. Decatur. After battle-readiness training, Morton deployed to the war zone, arriving in the winter of 1966. For the next six months, the ship made a significant contribution to the battle effort, firing more than ten thousand rounds in support of ground forces.

In the summer of 1966, I received orders to the U.S. Navy postgraduate school in Monterey, California. And after earning a masters degree in economics/systems analysis in July 1967, I was ordered to the Navy's Bureau of Naval Personnel in Washington, DC.

Following two years at Bupers I was sent to the Naval War College in Newport, Rhode Island, a place where I had already spent six years of my life. We lived in base quarters and the kids had a grand time. Though my wife and I never articulated that the Navy was our life's work, by this time we were quite happy with our career even though our lives were still bouncing about like ping pong balls.

I took my first creative writing course, published my first short story, "The Gig of the Morton Maru," and the writing bug hit me right where it should, in the muse.

Pop's MBSQS must have kicked in because, after learning that I had screened for command of a destroyer, I was ordered "in-country" Vietnam as an advisor to the Vietnamese Navy.

After specialized training in riverine-guerilla warfare followed by Survival, Escape, Rescue, and Evasion (SERE) training, I shipped out to become the senior advisor to the commanding officer of the Logistic Support Base (LSB) at Nha Be in the Rung Sat Special Zone (RSSZ).

Naval Advisory Team
Author kneeling in center with his combat sailors and marines as advisors in the Rung Sat Special Zone

Author (tall Navy officer on right) with Boy and Girl Scouts in Vietnamese Rung Sat village

The most distressing thing about going off to war is separation from the family. The kids didn't take my being in the war zone very well -- we had been on short duty for four years. My wife took it best. She had seen me come and go for over twenty years. It was a sad departure, lots of tears, and hugs, promises to write.

Shortly after taking command, I was ordered to "double hat" as senior advisor to the Vietnamese commanding officer of Rung Sat Special Zone. I was now commanding officer for the sailors and Marine advisors of one of the most unique places in all Vietnam. Our mission was to protect the ships on the Long Tau Channel, the very river that I had transited while in command of U.S.S. Cocopa in 1963 and about which I wrote not only a short history, but also a novel titled *The Advisor (Cô-Vân)*.

I flew about 80 combat chopper missions in protection of the Long Tau Channel and was shot at in that job. My enlisted sailor and Marine advisors did a superb job, contributing to control of the Viet Cong.

About every two or three weeks I would stay over in Saigon after a meeting and call the family at home, in the wee hours of the morning Vietnam time.

Another way my wife and I kept the kids in the loop was when we had our one-week Rest and Recreation (R&R). Barb and I met in Hawaii for a couple of days, then jumped a plane and finished the R&R at home with the kids. This was contrary to military rules, and when I passed through Hawaii on the way back to base, I thought I had bought the farm until I learned my boss, a rear admiral, had done exactly the same thing.

During the later stages of the war, the advisors turned over their boats and equipment and successfully trained the Vietnamese: Rung Sat Special Zone held until the very end. We flew home to the shouts of my sailors and Marines – my guys all came home alive.

On completion of in-country Vietnam duty, I proudly accepted command of U.S.S. Cook DE 1083, later FF 1083, a frigate named after my Annapolis classmate Wilmer Cook who had been shot down and lost over North Vietnam.

The Message of the Puzzle Ring

USS Cook FF 1083

Commanding U.S.S. Cook was almost as much fun as Cocopa. I had a good crew and a ship that was new, so I could do little wrong. The ship won every award and recognition available, especially those that had to do with people. When the new commander of the surface force asked me to join him on his staff, I could not refuse.

Next I was ordered to assistant chief of staff for plans and operations, Commander Cruiser Destroyer Group One (only nuclear powered ships). The day after Christmas of 1979, I received a phone call from the chief of staff. He had purposely refrained from calling until after Christmas in order not to spoil the day for the family. He asked if I could take emergency orders to relieve as skipper of U.S.S. Worden, CG-18, a guided missile cruiser home-ported in Yokosuka, Japan. The captain's wife had been diagnosed with cancer, and he had to get off as soon as possible to be with her.

My wife and I discussed the change. Two of our daughters were in college, one of whom was married. The move would interrupt our youngest daughter's high school, but how could I refuse helping an officer in trouble? Again MBSQS sat on the edge of my memory.

In less than two weeks I was flown to the Philippines, then to an aircraft carrier off Singapore, then transferred by chopper to the fantail of Worden. I relieved as skipper (I still cherish that title) three days later, and I believe the previous captain got back to his wife in time to comfort her.

USS Worden CG 18

Worden was the only cruiser home-ported in Asia. Consequently the ship was deployed from the foreign port of Yokosuka and underway more than 75 percent of the time. It was not conducive to family life, but we, my wife and our high school aged daughter muddled through.

In 1980, while on our way to the India Ocean to fight Iran, if necessary, and gain the release of our embassy personnel being held hostage, we deviated from course to investigate a small boat drifting at sea. I ordered our gig to investigate. To our dismay, 44 children were found stuffed in the bowels of the boat. We picked them up, fed them, examined their health, sank their boat, and took them with us to Singapore where they were all turned over to international organizations for placement.

The Message of the Puzzle Ring

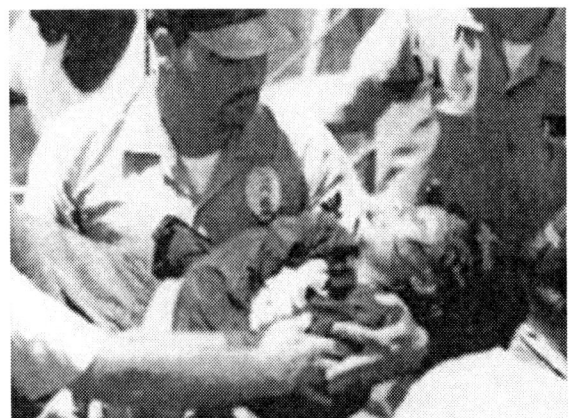

Photos of Vietnamese rescue

Carl. A. Nelson

Author

Shortly thereafter my time in the Navy was up. I had climbed my personal mountain, that of commanding a cruiser. Thirty-three years of service to the nation had been as interesting and exciting as any boy from Pittsburgh should be allowed to enjoy. I loved every minute of it.

Honored to command three fighting ships, I spent 13½ half years deployed at sea. I was in the Navy during the Korean War, the Cold War, and the Vietnam War; I had seen the Navy grow to greatness. Good people worked for me, and I worked for some very good men. I wanted sea duty and foreign places and ended up leaving the Navy I loved, holding my head high, a highly decorated Navy captain.

I had been in the Navy all my grown life and it was all I knew. My wife and I left the Navy with the same strong marriage we brought with us plus three wonderful daughters who gave us two grandchildren each. I achieved what I wanted and did it my way. I felt elated and proud. I had done my bit for Uncle Sam, left on my own terms, and was alive.

On the other hand I had lost my purpose. What would be my next life's work? Was I ready to test myself again? This was a major turning point. What would my life-long secret pal, Pop Ferger, recommend?

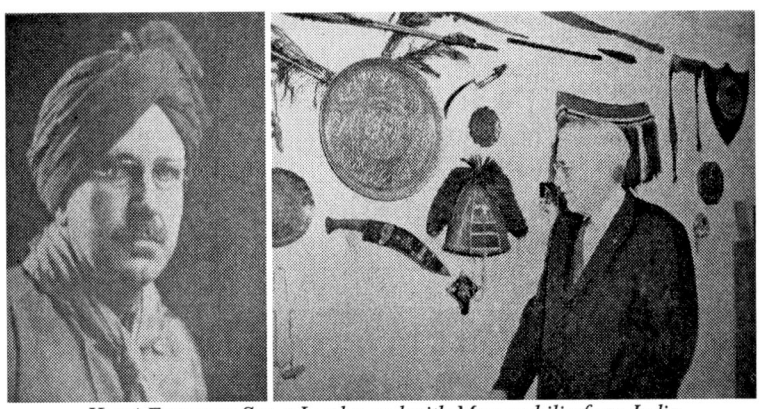

Henri Ferger as Scout Leader and with Memorabilia from India

Chapter 13

Finding Pop

In our American culture, if a man admires another man, it is unlikely the other will know it. Many thousands of years of male macho culture have painted out verbal expressions of that kind.

By now you know Pop Ferger was a man I admired, and for forty years he was and still is my secret pal, my conscience, my moral compass, my other dad. He didn't know it; I never told him.

I was very young when we met. Yet the Bible where he wrote about the four-square life beneath the passage in Luke 2:52 was with me everywhere I went in the Navy.

In the fall of 1981, I decided to leave the naval service to enter another phase of my life. Not knowing what course that might take, I again thought about Pop, the man who had impressed me so much and whose message had helped me through my failures and successes. Years had passed since we'd corresponded. I decided to look him up but had no idea where he might be. Would he still be in India?

I called James H. Graham, a Navy master chief for religious programs and technical advisor for the office of the Force Chaplain, Commander Naval Surface Force, San Diego. I asked if he could help.

"Give me a few days, sir."

Shortly I received a note. The master chief gave me the telephone number of the Union Theological Seminar (UTS) in New York. My phone call to the UTS library brought a copy of a page from the alumni catalogue for 1917 that outlined Pop's life from birth in 1889 including his career posts from 1910 through 1934.

I said to myself, *That's no help. Where is he now?*

I was rewarded with a notation from the Presbyterian Historical Society that he was in retirement to the small town of Dryden, New York.

In the spring of 1982, just after my retirement and not sure what to expect in return, I wrote a short note to Pop asking if he remembered me.

In less than a week, a long letter arrived. "Of course I remember you -- very well indeed, a lanky chap to whom I gave the name, 'Lamba Singh' - the first word meaning tall. We met in July 1943. You were the one who solved the puzzle ring. If you are ever near Dryden I would be pleased to see you."

Not bad for a man who is 93 years old, I told myself.

That next summer while in Pennsylvania staying with family, I called Pop and set up an appointment.

As I drove across New York on I-80 from Jamestown toward Dryden, I wondered about the interesting life Henri must have experienced in northern India and many other places. Doubts crept into my mind about going to visit him. Was I doing the right thing to search out and visit him after all these years? Was my connection to him simply a childish memory? After all, I was a retired Navy captain with a lot of life experiences. What could he do for me?

Putting away my doubts, I parked the car in front of an older home with a front porch and a high peaked roof, similar to many houses in that region. I cautiously climbed the steps and rang the doorbell. When he came to the door, I have to admit that my stomach churned a bit. He greeted me with, "Well… Lamba Singh, how long has it been? Let's see, 1943 to 83. Pretty close to 40 years." His eyes twinkled at his own joke. "Of course an Annapolis man knows how to add and subtract."

I took Pop's outstretched hand and squeezed as firmly as I could – I wanted him to know I was the man he wanted me to be.

"Hmm, strong grip," he said. "Well, come in and take that seat." He pointed to a lounge chair then took his seat directly in front of me on an ottoman.

He looked just as I thought he would. Tall, six feet or more, a bit slumped with age. His brown hair had turned grey (so had mine), yet he still wore a mustache, and his clear blue eyes pinched in humor still complemented a mind that sopped up information like a sponge.

"Tell me about you," he asked in the same voice and with eyes that I remembered from so long ago.

"Not much to tell. How are you, sir?" I asked.

"Oh, no you don't. I asked first," he said smiling. I was not surprised. He always wanted to know the other person's story, ducking his own.

"Since 1943? That's a long time, Pop."

"You're no longer in the Navy."

"True. Retired -- served 33 years."

"Long time."

"Not long enough – a young man's game. Everyone has to go sooner than later."

"You graduated Annapolis. Marvelous."

"Yes, sir, but not everything in my life went perfectly."

"Tell me about that."

"I had a few toe-stubbing problems along the way. Nothing…" I didn't want to begin a conversation with my stories.

"Doesn't seem the problems hurt you. After all, you are happily married with three daughters."

"True, sir. In the long run the problems were surmountable. I do have a marvelous family and had a wonderful career, very interesting and exciting."

"You commanded some of Uncle Sam's warships?"

"Yep. First was an ocean towing and salvage ship, then a frigate with a helicopter, and finally a guided missile cruiser. Had four tours of duty in the Vietnam War – one of them for a year on the ground where I commanded sailors and Marine advisors in the Mekong Delta region of South Vietnam, the Rung Sat Special Zone." My voice had a bragging tone, but I didn't care. I wanted to emphasize that I did OK.

"I usually don't pry… but I'm curious. Why didn't you stay in the Navy and become an admiral?"

I gave him my best smile. "Usually you don't pry and usually we don't talk about those things, but for my friend…" I paused. "Not every admiral in the Navy is ethical. Some focus on war fighting while others like to play."

"Hmm…" He changed the subject. "Have you kept in touch with the other boys who were with you at Camp Greenwood?"

"No, sir. Navy got in the way."

"They're all doing well," Pop said.

"You kept in touch?"

I was amazed to hear him spout off their names, "Yes. Besides you, there was Don Williams, Doug Bowman, Ralph Krishbaum, Donald Shaw, John Smith, and Roy Eichman – Roy became the pastor of his own church – and the other one – his name escapes me."

After forty years he can't remember just one?

"All right, your turn." I laughed. "What have you been up to? I've read your letters and know all your secrets."

"Well, since you know so much, do you know that on October 27, 1959, Kitty and I returned to the USA after almost 50 years in India."

"Where is she?"

"Off for the afternoon with her church friends."

"I was hoping to meet her. But go on, sir, what else have you been doing?"

"For a few months I raked leaves and tended the house. But I soon became busier than ever after taking up a new career as a photographer."

"Your letters about your travels are marvelous."

"Thank you. I do like to see foreign places. Been around the world eight times."

"Eight times? Do you and Kathryn miss India? I asked.

"Oh, heavens, yes. That's our other home. It's where our heart is. We love the people. It's the land where the heart is king. That's one of my favorite photos, I had a reunion with my first Indian Boy Scouts" He pointed to the picture shown below:

Rev.H. R. Ferger with Dehra Scouts, 31 December 1964
Pop is shown in the front row, second from the right.

"Did you ever get to India?" he asked.

"No, sir. Practically everywhere else, but the Navy never saw fit to send me to that country. Still want to."

I then asked the question I had driven so far to ask, "What do you think I should I do now? All I know is Navy – 33 years, nothing else." I threw it at him as if it were a baseball player's last pitch for a no-hitter.

"Did you forget the four foundations of a well-rounded four-square life? Don't tell me you've forgotten. You still have the Bible and the puzzle ring?"

"The Bible – I take it with me, always.

You're not wearing your puzzle ring."

"It's still in the family. As a matter of fact, everyone has a ring."

"Good for you."

"When I was younger I wore it all the time. Not much into jewelry – Navy regs… I still remember the message – MBSQS -- Mind, Body, Social Qualities, Spirit."

"Good. Clever abbreviation. Your life has not been lived by accident. Neither was Jesus' life. You've been serving your country in the military. And you did well, seems without regrets. Maybe Luke 2.52 helped."

"You're fishing, sir."

"Of course," He smiled. "That's what I still do. I'm still a preacher, remember."

"And my answer is that it made a big difference. Not the solution for everything, but was always helped me through the tough times. Now I'm stuck. What to do next."

What do *you* think your next life's work should be?"

"Don't know."

Hi voice dropped to a whisper as if he was reluctant to speak. "Ah… ah, have you reconciled with your father?"

"Yes, somewhat. Before his death – lung cancer – I spent time with him. We came to terms."

"How about your mother and brother Gordon?"

The Message of the Puzzle Ring

"Mom is doing OK. I see her often. My brother is doing terrific. Graduated from Pitt, served in the Army, and has a good career in the car business."

Like the pastor he was, his hand went to my shoulder. It was as if we had never parted. Like the father I hardly had, he shook his head, "Well, don't look back. You served your country well. Now keep aiming high! Think of this as a time for fulfillment of your dreams. Life is full of things that need to be done. Have I told you what my friend and hero Mohandas Mahatma Gandhi said? Did I tell you I knew him in India." He paused, then quietly quoted, "'Whatever you do will seem insignificant, but it is most important that you do it. One must *be* the change one wishes to see in the world.'" Pop smiled and said, "Gandhi was a great man. You'll find it... your new life's work. Think hard about the foundations of a four-square life: What are your strengths and weaknesses? Are you prepared to take the message a step farther?"

There was a moment of silence while I thought about how to answer him ... his words jarred me so much that I couldn't answer. I swallowed hard ... finally I said, "Ah... what did you mean are you prepared to take the message a step farther?"

"Well, MBSQS is for you, for your growth, but there are things you can do for others, the larger world."

"Well, I'm thinking about becoming a writer like you ... but one who concentrates on international themes. I've even started a novel about the Vietnam War."

"Sounds like a marvelous idea – you know a lot about that. When will it be ready for me to read?"

"I just started." I felt my face flush at the thought.

He said, "I never wrote for publication, although several of my articles have been in newspapers and magazines."

I then told him my story about the time when returning from a fly fishing trip in Oregon, that my wife (who was driving) asked me what I wanted to do next.

I responded, "I think I'll try writing."

"Writing?" The tome of her voice rose. She came very close to losing control of the car. "You don't know anything about writing!"

"Well," I held up a tablet of lined paper. "I'm writing a short story about fishing for Steelhead trout on the Umpqua River. When we get home you can type it up, we'll send it off to a magazine and make a lot of money."

She half turned to me, her face red with impatience and hurt. "You have me mixed up with one of your Navy yeomen. You better learn how to type."

I smiled.

Pop's face broke out in a smile. "Spunky girl!"

"She was right and she's fine with it now I did learn how to type, but I'm still ambivalent about writing."

His laughter spread to his eyes. I knew he had a sense of humor and collected jokes, so I was not surprised when he said, "Have I told you the story about Dr. Simpson who had treated a man's wife who subsequently died. The doctor got the following note from the widower. "My wife has departed to regions above. For your help in this matter, I send you my hearty thanks."

We both laughed until he said, "One of the reasons I still love Kitty after 68 years is she still permits me a few jokes now and then."

Again there was a pause as if we had run out of things to say. Then I asked. "Tell me more about you. Your life?"

True to his humble nature, he skipped over the many details, much of which I already knew from his letters. He apologized that Kitty was away. "She has arthritis -- we live next to our son John and his wife Martha. He's a physician and takes good care of us. We have supper with them and their children almost every evening. We're well cared for." He repeated.

"Do you still march in the Princeton parade?"

"Oh, yes, and my goal is to live long enough to be the oldest alumni to pass in review."

"Tell me, how did your Indian boys respond to Luke 2:52 ... your message?"

"Fairly well, I believe. Particularly those who were Boy Scouts. One never knows what they will be like until they grow up, like you."

Then his eyes burned in glittery brightness. "Let us pray." And he bowed his head. The words came easy to this man who believed.

We shook hands when we parted. This time I was more gentle than when I first greeted him several hours before. I didn't want to leave the comfortable feelings and warmth of being with my friend.

I drove away from Dryden very fulfilled. I had found Pop and it was good. He was still the generous optimist I remembered from my boyhood – the secret pal of my life. And he did it again... he left me with a complex thought...
Are you prepared to take the message a step farther?

Receiving Doctorate

Chapter 14
New Life's Work (New Horizons)

Starting over in my fifties was like being drawn to a foreign place that I always longed for. I admit it was a bit scary to think I could do something else. I knew I wanted to challenge myself to try something totally new, something I always wanted to do, but what? After thirty-three years as a surface warfare officer in the United States Navy, I realized I knew nothing about my own country. Now I had the freedom to explore and assess its riches.

All I knew was my hair was gray, I was a bit heavier, and doing something different while learning about America was my challenge. The Navy had consumed my life. As a result I had a very narrow point of view. I knew nothing else. As a family we had lived on the fringes of America – east and west coasts, reading newspapers, watching TV, but never really living in our own culture. We lived on or near naval bases and communities dominated by military. We had our own grocery store (commissary), gas station, and department store.

According to novelist F. Scott Fitzgerald, "There are no second acts in American lives." Maybe so, but many people try. They just have to, because they're drawn to test themselves once again. They believe it's never too late to grow.

Pop told me to follow his message and not look back. "Aim high," he said.

I thought about that during my flight from New York to California. I said to myself, *MBSQS worked once. Why not again?* The same opportunities that came to me during my first life's work could work twice.

But what would I do?

After that visit with Pop I decided to take a chance.

Several friends told me there was not enough time in my life to start a new adventure. But I knew that was what I wanted to do was something completely different. I loved the Navy but now I wanted to taste civilian life, politics, art, local civics, business, and the like: I wanted to experience the 'whole enchilada.' But whatever I chose as my next life's work, I wanted it to be something that would keep me busy for the rest of my life and to make a small contribution.

By my calculations, I had more than enough income, the mortgage was paid, and the kids were almost finished college. Why not take a risk?

I decided to challenge myself. Do I have talents? I could try something entirely new, test my right brain, my creative side. Maybe I could become a writer or a painter, something I always wanted to try. I didn't know much about anything except the Navy. But I could learn." I told my wife I'd already started writing a novel based on my Vietnam War experiences.

"When can I read it?" she asked.

I felt relieved. Apparently she accepted my skills at learning new things. She quickly became my best and only supporter.

While on active duty I wrote several non-fiction articles that had been published in a military magazine. I had even written and had published a short story or two. All I knew was that words came easily to me on paper, even though I still wasn't much of a talker. The writing bug bit me sometime in my past, maybe as early as when I wrote my final paper at the Naval Academy, and I had taken a course in creative writing while a student at the War College. Pop's letters about India certainly could also have been the genesis. I found myself driven to get up early to put words on paper. The creative process fascinated me.

I began this new life's purpose in earnest. I wanted to write for a broad international audience; after all, I had spent my life, to the present, out and about in the world. I invested in a computer, went back to high school to learn how to type, and began taking writing courses from a delightful woman teacher at a local community college. I attended a conference of writers in Santa Barbara and even tried reading some of my war novel to other wannabe writers. I had to catch up with those who'd majored in liberal arts and English. I bootstrapped my writing education by reading lots of books and by finishing the war novel, rewriting it again and again until it was publishable.

After my demanding life in the Navy, I found that writing did not fill my day. Though the California lifestyle was great: golf, swimming and relaxing on the patio, editing my drafts and reading the books of other writers became stifling. I became restless. I took several more courses at the local community college and found that I could sit in a classroom and enjoy the company of younger students. So back to school I went.

I took several tests and submitted my transcripts, and voila! I was accepted for a doctorate in business administration, finding that specializing in international economics and trade appealed to me. In less than two years, I graduated with my doctorate in finance (international trade emphasis). My dissertation about exporting products of small- to medium-size businesses subsequently sold to a major publisher and became a best seller. It has continued to sell for over twenty years.

I returned to my war novel, *The Advisor (Cô-Vân)*. After that I moved into non-fiction, publishing seven books about international trade. I even experimented with playwriting and poetry and wrote two more novels, all of which won honors. It's as if something was driving me to succeed: could it be MBSQS?

I found that teaching courses in my field of international business suited me, so I kept my hand in, at first teaching at several local universities and eventually settling in with a professorship at a small California international business university.

Writing and teaching opened doors to other aspects of civilian life including religion and politics, those things that can make a contribution to peoples lives.

What have I learned while ageing? You should continue to have goals and strike out to achieve them. It is not enough to fold up the tent in your fifties believing life is over. As Pop said, "Never look back!"

As a result of MBSQS and my civilian experiences, I've become a humanist-social-liberal with philosophical leanings toward a more peaceful world. I have seen the wretched and appalling conditions after World War II in Europe in the late fifties. It was not until I saw Japan, the

Philippines, and South Vietnam in 1963-64, and Taiwan, South Korea, and Hong Kong in 1965-66 that I realized how far behind those countries were. If we could only rid ourselves of war and transfer the mechanism of industrial economic development across the world, everyone could live a better life. Why not?

Do you remember the Vietnamese boat people we picked up at sea in 1980? Fourteen years later the leader of those we rescued wrote a statement in Vietnamese and presented it to me. This is the translation.

Moline, April 5, 89
Dear Captain Carl Nelson,

No word could describe how happy I am to know that you are back in the U.S. and well since that special event on the Pacific Ocean where you brought us to the free land by the U.S.S. Worden -- April 1980.

Again, on behalf of the 44 people on that little boat, and myself -- I, with deep gratitude from the bottom of my heart, thank you very much for your kind assistance which I will never forget -- without it, I don't know what my life will end up.

My family and I are more than happy to hear from you and may be a wonderful visit that you can arrange in the nearest future to this area where I'm enjoying life in this great country. We look forward to hear from you soon.

Sincerely Yours,

Tinh Hoang

"One of the luckiest boat people"

PS. It's going to be great to have you and yours coming here so we can recall a lot of things."

Looking back, it's obvious how I've changed. My life has had two parts: war (33 years) and international peace (27 years). I give credit to MBSQS for motivating me to aim high, but more so to try another life's work, to take the message a step further -- that of opening others' eyes to the modern integration, merging, and melding of the people on our globe.

Chapter 15
Facing Painful Times

Despite the positive theme of this book, that is, modeling your life after Jesus and rising to do useful work, there are times when one might ask, *God, where are you? Don't you see that I'm grieving? You must not be paying attention to me and my life. Why else would you let this happen? After all, I do try to live as a four-square person using MBSQS!*

Painful times: death, failure, mistakes -- can come in small pieces or large, often more frequently than we believe that we can weather. The message, MBSQS, even though it helps fortify our inner strength, isn't a guaranteed path to deal with all of life's bum deals.

Even Reverend Henri suffered several rough patches on his road to Heaven. His advantage was that he could always lean on the Bible to help him bring strength to others.

One of those cruel times happened in 1923, seven years before I was born and a few months after Henri contracted typhoid. As his doctor ordered, he spent time recovering in Kashmir. Coincidently, Henri's father (Pappa), mother, and sister Margaret left Chattanooga in January 1921 for a year's trip around the world. After visiting Paris, Italy, Greece, Egypt, and the Holy Land, they reached India in April 1922. They spent that summer with Henri, Kitty, and family members Nellie and Wirth, in the famed Vale of Kashmir, the beautiful valley lying between the Great Himalayas and the Pir Panjal range. Afterwards, Henri's parents and sister continued on to Java, China, Korea, and Japan.

It was on the homeward leg of their trip from Hawaii, in January of 1923, that the unbelievable happened. Pappa contracted pneumonia and died suddenly. Henri's mother succumbed to the same disease the following month.

No book can outline what to do when one loses both parents at practically the same time. (See Appendix E for a complete discussion about the Ferger family.)

In terrible grief, Pop and Kitty had to rise to the situation. Strengthened by their faith and the spiritual element of the MBSQS message, their life's work in India took a back seat. Duty called. They immediately went on furlough and returned to the States to take care of affairs. For a time they stayed at the Ferger home at 830 Vine Street, but after things were resolved in Chattanooga, they went on to New York. Henri renewed his contacts at the Union Seminary and took some training at the New York Institute of Photography.

After the birth of their son John on January 12, 1924, and when it was safe for Kitty to travel, they returned to India. Henri assumed the post of principal of the American Presbyterian Missionary School in Jhansi. From then on the Fergers' life became one of alternating long periods in education and missionary work separated my short furloughs in the USA.

After they retired and settled in Dryden, New York, Pop was tested again. His Kittydear died at age 95 on May 5, 1982. They had been together for 67 years. Their lives were so interesting and intertwined that they had no time to complain. Though slowed by arthritis and other ailments, Kathryn did volunteer work with the local church.

Before her death, Henri continued his world travels and kept busy in their American home. After she died he acted, according to daughter-in-law Martha Ferger, "somewhat matter-of-fact about it." He alone would have known all the hardships Kathryn endured as the wife of a missionary: Cultural changes, strange food, but always remaining compassionate in every sense of the word. Of course Reverend Henri would have spent long periods praying and communing with her.

I imagine him saying something like, *I'll be along to join you soon, Kittydear.*

*****

For me the most painful day of my life was in 2004 when my wife died of lung cancer. She was only 72. We were married 48 years and engaged for 2 1/2. I had known her since we were children.

Before her death my emotions were bottled – a survival strategy going back to my dad's defection. For most of my life I lived in a military society where showing emotions was not permitted, like the line in the movie, "There's no crying in baseball!" During the care-giving period leading up to my wife's death, I fought the idea that there was no cure. *She would not die*, I said to myself. *There must be some curative prize for a person like her.*

After her death I went into a tailspin, a devastating deep depression – terrible, raw grief with lots and lots of tears and snot. I consulted Pop's message in my Bible, but nothing helped me. My pastor John Giffin recommended therapy.

My wife had stopped smoking about fifteen years earlier, yet for most of the year before she was diagnosed with lung cancer, she had been coughing. The cough was low grade and dry. It wasn't until the fall of 2002, after a 19-day tour of Europe, that her pulmonary specialist discovered a malignant tumor in the lower left lobe. He candidly, some would say brutally, told us that the average life for someone with her disease was two years.

I remember choking back my feelings as we drove home. I didn't want to believe her doctor. Inside I felt sick because I knew about lung cancer. It is the most deadly of the cancers.

She elected to do everything possible. She was the fighter. I was the wimp.

The tumor couldn't be resected, so she agreed immediately to radiation and chemo treatments.

In less than the two years her pulmonary specialist had prophesized, the waiting was over. The doctors had tried everything, but on the 19th of August 2004 we started hospice and one month later, on the 18th of September, my "love" Barbara Long died.

For her, a brave and generous Navy wife who lived as an exceptional human being – wife, lover, friend, mother, grandmother, what else could she have done? Her life's work was her family.

I hadn't thought about bereavement until it struck me that she was really gone. I told myself that MBSQS hadn't worked for me. What good was it if I couldn't save my wife?

I knew I couldn't stay in our empty house, so I packed up and began what I call my "drive and cry" road trip. I took along my Bible, read the chapter of Luke over and over, especially 2:52, and thought about Pop Ferger.

Now all at once my bottled-up emotions came. I felt like there was a deep hole in my chest; it heaved, and the tears flowed like spring water over a riffle on a stony stream. I wanted her to be waiting for me around the next bend in the river, in the passenger seat next to me, in the room when I returned. She wasn't, but I still wished for that.

I originally intended to drive north to Oregon and fly-fish for Steelhead trout in the North Umpqua River, but after about 12 days, many imagined talks with Pop, I felt my wife calling me to return. Thinking I was ready for the empty house, I cut short from my intended two-week search.

When I reached home it hit me. She wasn't there. I shouted anyway, as I had a thousand times before, "Honey, I'm home."

I thought I had sufficiently recovered from her loss, but I had not. It felt like a blindside hit on a football field, again devastated by the grief.

I went searching for more answers. I asked friends who'd had this same experience. Their words only confirmed my need to find help. My grief continued, and I found myself sobbing at the slightest thought of her, the mention of her name, a sound, a memory.

What would Pop Ferger have told me? I knew what he would say, "Go to church, pray."

I joined a group having the same trouble, that is wanting to understand what was happening in their minds. The facilitator, a woman who specializes in grief recovery, asked us, as a homework assignment, to think about the difference between a thought and a feeling. Her question involved trying to understand the causes of grief and depression. Is there a connection between thoughts and feelings, and does one affect the other?

She gave us a list of 21 feelings including anger, depression, fear, feeling lost, guilt, helplessness, loneliness, preoccupation, sadness, shame, and yearning. I experienced them all.

She asked us to explore just one part of our feelings.

Then she questioned, "What three things about your loss are on your mind right now?"

My answer was, "I miss her. I feel terribly lonely. I'm confused. I feel empty. Can I fill the void?"

Although I have faith that God has reasons for everything, I found myself exploring my confusion. Where was Pop Ferger and MBSQS when I needed them most? In the past my referral to Luke 2:52 was quiet and always unseen. Now, I felt like I must shout for help. I talked to Pop as though he were beside me and asked him what to do.

Soon my feelings of depression and sorrow for myself, changed to feelings of good fortune. How grateful I was to have known my wife, let alone to be married to her, for 48 years. I could have married a spoiled, whiny, demanding person.

She was so brave. Sure, she questioned and had moments of fear, but she accepted death. She told me it was okay to cry. I held her, read the Bible to her, and told her that I would love her always but I couldn't stop death from happening.

What now?

At a group therapy session, one of the members, when she learned that we had been married for 48 years and that I had known my wife since she was about seven or eight years old, asked me, "And you still liked her?"

My first reaction was that her question was rude. It was like a sharp needle or a stick in my eye. If she were a man I would have challenged him, maybe slapped him, and told him his remark was stupid. Then I thought, giving her the benefit of my doubt, that she must have been trying to be funny and missed the mark. I suppose there are people who live with a spouse they no longer like, but how could she know that my wife and I liked each other always and seldom disagreed.

Tough times happen. They are not always associated with death. In addition to losing my wife, I had been crushed by the loss of my father to alcohol, time in a Marine brig, losing a year of my life to academics, and closing out a first life's work that I loved.

It's clear to me now that people who haven't experienced grief can't understand it. I learned that one must go through adversity in order to come back and ultimately reach the success of MBSQS. It's how you conduct yourself in defeat that makes you grow. Pop didn't capture me with Christianity. He caught me with the Christ-like image of perfection.

My brother, Gordon, who was eight years old at the time, had met Pop Ferger when he came to our home on Dartmore Street back in 1943, wrote me a letter. In it he recalled that once in my life, way back then, that I stated my childhood dream, "Before I die, it's India for me."

His suggestion was that this might be the right time to experience Pop's life in the place he loved so much.

Wow! I said to myself. *My bro is so right.*

Come along with me. I'm off to India!

Chapter 16
India - My Boyhood Dream

During my many years in the Navy and even the extensive traveling I've done in my second career as author and professor, I had yet to fulfill my dream to visit India, the mysterious land of my boyhood, imagining the places Pop Ferger described so eloquently in his letters.

I decided to accept my brother's wisdom and go to India in February 2005. My reservation was for an eighteen-day tour of North India, the region where Pop had served for 50 years. My original purpose was to see the country for myself and at the same time break the shackles of grief. I asked several friends and relatives if they would join me as a traveling companion. No takers.

My mind was pretty much made up. I would travel alone. Then I remembered Dolores Hansen, the widow of my Annapolis classmate who'd visited our home from time to time when she was in San Diego. She lived in Utah so Barbara and I had only casually kept in touch, mostly relaying jokes and other light things that came by Internet.

When she jokingly told me in an E-mail that she was broke and paying off her credit card debt from a summer trip to Europe with her children, I told her that was too bad, otherwise she could join me on my pending tour through India. I was completely surprised when she came back a few days later. Her E-mail said, "I'm interested, but I need more information about suitable arrangements."

Guilt.

I didn't really know her. She seemed to be a nice person, smart, Ph.D. in education, elementary school principal. But who knows what people are really like until one has spent time and seen all sides of his or her personality? On the other hand, a traveling companion could be just a friend, and over time I could run into another person just as pleasing.

My children knew I was off to India, but I had not told them about my new traveling partner. Before her death, Barbara had talked to me about life after she was gone. She told me I should marry again, that is, if I found the right person. I didn't want to talk about it.

I called a meeting with the girls to break my news. To my surprise, all the girls had talked with their mother about me and told me that mother wanted me to remarry. Each of my daughters had been twice divorced and remarried and, knowing that divorce and death are similar, they accepted my situation, even comforted me by saying they were good with it.

I now had a three-fold purpose for the trip. First, I wanted to see the landscape and sense what Pop experienced. Second, as a professor of international business, I wanted to observe the economy of the world's largest democracy and second-most-populous nation. Mentally I would compare its progress since the time Pop was there. Lastly, I wanted to know if I would be comfortable with another woman.

As you have already learned, during his 50 years of service to his mission, Henri witnessed the greatest change in modern Indian history. In his letters he portrayed images of India, a place teeming with humans all struggling to survive. He described the sounds of stringed instruments, horns, beggars, hawkers, smells of burning dung and incense. He warned of the disturbing sights of bodies floating in Mother Ganges and young girls carrying dirty infants slung on their hips as they begged for rupees in the streets of every town. He explained that because many Indians speak three languages, Hindi, Urdu, and English (to do business), he had to become fluent in Hindi, less so in Urdu, more popular among Muslims in the North.

I had been told that Delhi was different, that it was not India, but I had to see for myself. Pop had spent a great deal of time in that city, and I wanted to see through his eyes. I found a country that is hot, humid, and beggar-poor with cows wandering the same streets as poor mothers holding tiny naked babies. Today's population of more than a billion people is up from about 1.9 million in Pop's day.

In addition to Delhi, we toured six other cities and many of the roads in between by air, train, and van, seeing small villages, large cities, and middle-income suburbs.

Dolores and I visited the Red Fort and the Ganges. My heart was full at the Taj Mahal, a place that touched me greatly because my nerves were still very raw. I had a mystical experience there: It seemed I was in connection with both my wife and Pop. It became my favorite place in that country, maybe the world.

During our visit we observed many of the same images Pop wrote about, but the picture today is different. We saw snake charmers and monkeys on a leash, beggars still roaming streets with hands outstretched.

India is no longer a maelstrom of discontent. It is changing as we read. Its leadership has focused on the future and growth. One sign of a new India are the ring roads built around the major cities and the venture capital or risk investments that are everyday phrases in the lexicon of

Indian business. I found Hindus to be energetic and entrepreneurial, up early looking to make a buck (rupee) any way they can.

Bollywood has become the world's largest exporter of movies. The Indian technical schools turn out students known worldwide for their math and computer skills. India is a nation with a strategy for entrepreneurship, self-sufficiency, and intentions to be a full partner in the global economy. They are attaining their goals by manufacturing their own televisions, automobiles, and outsourcing their labor to foreign manufacturers.

How did this modern economic turn-around happen?

The Freedom Movement was started by the modern forefathers Mahatma Gandhi, the Nehru dynasty, and many other stalwarts like Motilal Nehru, Valiabhai Patel, and Moulana Abdul Gazad during the pre-independence days. But the more recent upturn in the economy is due to the "liberalization" movement which started in 1991-1992, when Lai Bahadur Shastri became Prime Miinister and reformed (almost abolished) the licensing procedure for foreign direct investments, opening the economy to global competition and the beneficial consequences that followed. This is evident in the remarkable upward growth rate of the GDP and gross capital formation. (See Appendix B for more details.)

Caste barriers are softening. The law forbids the system, but in truth India's culture continues with three castes, three major religions, and many languages and cultures. Some preferences are reserved for the lowest levels of Indian society so they can have equal opportunities to rise. College is for all castes; mass education programs are in place with growing equality for women. We saw modern malls on the outskirts of cities where teen-age kids hang out just like in America and Europe. Cell phones are everywhere, and there is a growing population of car owners.

My dream was fulfilled late in life, and it turned out to be one of my richest experiences.

I do believe that Pop would be pleased with the changes Dolores and I found. Standing on Indian soil, I wondered if Hindu and Muslim boys were just as inspired by Henri's four-square message as I was. I hypothesized that he might deserve a bit of recognition for his contribution to India's change.

How could that be?

Henri loved India so much that he stayed for fifty years and returned several times as a guest. His letters revealed that his real mission was his passion to give his boys a message that would help them develop into well-rounded,

```
                    ┌─────────────────────────┐
                    │   Take Pop's Message    │
                    │     a Step Farther      │
                ┌───┴─────────────────────┬───┘
                │  Act Morally, Ethically │
            ┌───┴──────────────────┬──────┘
            │   Adapt to Change    │
        ┌───┴─────────────────┬────┘
        │   Visualize Goals   │
   ┌────┴────────────────┬────┘
   │    Begin MBSQS      │
   └─────┬───────────────┴──────────────┐
         │   Stepping Stones of Life    │
         └──────────────────────────────┘
```

Chapter 17

Yesterday's Wisdom for Today's World

In 1951, when I was twenty years old and very much ashamed of having been punished with three days on bread and water in a brig guarded by Marines, I swore to seek a path that would change my life. I told myself that I wasn't a criminal -- I just did dumb things. I called it, "going through my stupid stage."

I promised never to let my friends and shipmates down again.

For most of my life I communicated with Pop, my secret pal, solely by letters, mostly his. That his message MBSQS stayed with me is an understatement, but I didn't always understand how it linked to Jesus. How could I succeed if I didn't understand Pop's message? How does it work? How does it give confidence and determination to achieve anything?

Today it's clear that I turned to rebellion and misbehavior in grade school, high school, and somewhat beyond, mostly against the wrong person, my mother. But I had no way to find my father and tell him what a crumb he was. So I reached back to Pop Ferger's puzzle ring and his four MBSQS words. Guess what? My life began to change.

A mentor like Pop can show us what's possible in the world. Look around at what's right in life, especially in America. Open your possibilities by envisioning goals.

I'm not a psychologist; all I can vouch for is my extensive life experience. Having graduated from boot camp and the Naval Academy as well as serving on the faculties of Annapolis, West Point, and commanding several Navy ships, I know this: Pop's wisdom is still very useful as it stands. It worked for me as the path to my goal to become a better person.

Pop developed his message sometime in the early 1900's, and today, in the twenty-first century, many things have changed. To rise in the constantly-changing circumstances of our continually-shifting world means Pop's four foundation words, MBSQS, must remain timeless because they get us started in our quest for a four-square life.

To reach the full potential offered by Pop's message, we must dig deeper to find the supplemental ideas that keep his message multi-generational and adapted to life today. We must think critically about the changes much as the curious boy Jesus did in the temple as written in Luke 2:52. He would have figured this out. After all, He did live a multifaceted life.

In Pop's day most people would be quite happy to find work right in their own back yards. Today rise means to climb a ladder, seek a higher position of leadership in your life's work.

Rising is often guided by intuition learned along the way. We must believe our life is our own yet keep in mind that we *do* need guidance from parents and other adults.

In my case, MBSQS gave me opportunities and pointed the direction to what I could achieve. I learned that doors opened for the four-square ☐, well-rounded person. Opportunities jumped at me; good things happened. Today the process is more complex. We must supplement and adat the four words with an understanding of today's issues.

"MIND - Mentally Awake"
Whatever you do, keep in mind that America was once an agrarian society. We were farmers with less need for a formal education. Since then we have gone through the industrial revolution and are now in the age of high technology.

Today the people of earth must adapt to globalism. We travel and trade as if 200 nations were in our back yard. Cultures are merging, as are languages. We emigrate to the jobs. Universities are rethinking their curricula to suit a changing interdisciplinary world that emphasizes the new global economy and new technologies, coupled with right brain thinking, enterprise, creativity, and innovation.

How will you deal with this challenge?

Pop would say, "Stay tuned."

"BODY - Physically Strong"
Exercise and games can contribute to a healthy body, but in modern life addiction to drugs, alcohol, and Internet video games including pornography are seductively sapping the strength of people worldwide as well as the nations where they live. It is too easy to find the "s…" as it called on the street and very hard to overcome. If you're into drugs, GET OUT! NOW! Don't be stupid. Drugs can affect your body, your mind, and your children, present and future. Alcohol is the number one family wrecker, period! Temper your life with a thoughtful lifestyle that includes good judgment, fitness, and plenty of rest.

"SOCIAL QUALITIES -- Do Others Like You?"

Pop's guidance was true and strong for his time. But the world has changed. Social qualities today include leadership, understanding globalism, and modern communications -- including social communications methods (Twitter, FaceBook, E-mail). The Internet can bring people and their cultures together to do good. Yet we can be challenged to join gangs, become bullies, exceed sexual boundaries, and ignore cultural ethics.

Social qualities include character, self-esteem, quality of life, loyalty, conduct, courtesy, kindness, and likeability.

Be secure in your manhood or womanhood and ask yourself where you want to be when you're 50 years old.

"SPIRIT -- Morally Straight"

Today Pop's spiritual guidance would be somewhat more complicated, yet it would still be based on caring about your fellow man. He would caution us to be careful of the three witches: lust for war; lust for power; lust for profit. He would tell us to gauge ethical and moral dilemmas against MBSQS and its Bible reference.

AVOIDING PITFALLS

What happens if you fail?

Failure is a part of life. Few of us escape a backward step sometime in our short lives on earth. If your life takes you to a point of recklessness -- a crevasse or precipice, physical or moral -- pause and consider the implications. Should you jump in, cross over, or turn away? What would your most trusted mentors want you to consider?

If you slip, like I did, rely on your will power as well as your family and social support to get back on track, to make something of yourself and hold the line toward the goal.

(See the Guide with Helps in Appendix H.)

[A letter] To Carl Nelson
Photo taken when teaching a small boy at Lume, Togo.
HR Ferger (Circa 1985)

Chapter 18

My Last Letter to Pop

Having always felt unworthy and ashamed that I knew Pop Ferger but corresponded so little, I finally sat down and penned the letter I should have written long ago.

Dear Pop:
I know that you died in 1989. You lived to be 100 years, wow! I learned about your passing from your son John.

How did I feel? You always asked me that...

Some might just shake their heads, say a short prayer, and move on; however, you never did that. You touched my soul forever, in the summer of 1943.

You were an educator, a missionary, a world traveler, and a photographer. With your brilliant mind, you could have done anything, yet you chose to serve Christ. Of course you saw yourself as a disciple and a messenger, but your heart was always open to young people, showing them how to strive to be a Christ-like, four-square person.

It took me a long time to grasp your message, but I finally got it and will pass it on. I have written this book about your life and in doing so discovered what I think is the true value of your message: It's a shorthand guide for living a good life which can serve as a motivational tool to help people become better. MBSQS just sits quietly on the shoulder, like Jiminy Cricket from Pinocchio, waiting for the right moment to whisper, "Yep, that's OK; or No, don't do that, or what would Jesus do? Or even, what would Pop Ferger do?"

I've learned that if we keep your message in our hearts and minds, it can sustain us during difficult times of growth and strife. It can help us better our lives by rising to our chosen position or life's work.

The Bible and other books help us. The Book of Psalms has many verses about choices, as does Proverbs, but for most young people in today's fast-moving world culture, those books are too long. People no longer carry their Bibles to work or school. I believe you knew that modern youngsters and adults would need something that is handy, like the puzzle ring and the lesson about living four-square, a message for all seasons.

I've learned that the power of the puzzle ring message is its simplicity. Today's boys and girls do need a short reference -- one that can help them make decisions quickly.

MBSQS outlines an optimistic, positive thinking process that helps those who have life issues and want to rise above their circumstances and get started in a four-square life. I believe that your message points us toward a new definition of man- and woman-hood. For a true sense of fulfillment, modern people are looking for more than just money and security. The message points us toward finding our life's work.

I've learned that your simple message cannot help us solve every problem. But it can be our foundation -- a way to help us think before making a mistake. Better yet, it gives us a way of getting back on track after we screw up. It can lead us back to a better way.

I consider myself one of the luckiest persons for having met you; the result was rising above my circumstances. At first I couldn't get MBSQS out of my mind. Later it would fade one day and come back the next. But once I got it, my life has been a grand adventure.

Every letter you sent from India was full of facts, but underneath there was energy – an expectation to do things – to get "off the couch." I believe that MBSQS can speak especially to dysfunctional people, the "woe is me" crowd who, when they are down, won't or can't get up and on their feet.

Just knowing you helped me become more considerate, not lash out or be hostile and angry, though I still do that occasionally. I've learned to be more concerned for the poor, strangers, widows and orphans, and to be more generous. Ethics, concern for others, and good humor are qualities that can be learned.

I've found that too many people fail to understand the extent of an adult's influence on young people, especially boys.

That was me when I was twelve. I was essentially without a father, and it took less than a week for you to hook me with your puzzle ring and message. I didn't care about the message then, but the ring was mine. Over time your MBSQS message did take hold, giving me confidence to go into the darkness of decision-making and overcome the fear of trying new things. It gave me the courage, when things didn't work out, to get up and get on my feet.

Finally, it made me think of balance -- the four-square life.

Your message taught me that if you know in yourself that your life is lacking something important and you seem to be stuck with no progress, you are probably ready to take the first step. Even if we don't have a clue what God is, we may be ready for the journey into our own humanity. The more human we are, the more God-like we are. The genius of God is that He has given us examples like Gandhi and yourself, Henri Ferger.

During your lifetime your four-square message must have reached thousands of boys: Hindus, Muslims, and American. Like many couriers, you will never know the effectiveness of your message, but the people who read this story will know its value.

Who knows how many lives you influenced during your travels across India as well as America? The numbers who came under your tutelage on two continents are untold. I'm still not sure which had the greater influence on me, you or your message.

How can I sum up your value?

I have no right to ask that question, but I do know that you, Henri Rabb "Pop" Ferger, were a great leader and also a great teacher.

What separates ordinary leaders or teacher from great ones? They don't just lead or teach; they inspire. What made you great were your message and your life-long mission to help young people rise.

You were a Christian from the beginning and practiced your religion continuously to the end. You set your mind, early on, to do God's work, and you did it 'til you could do no more.

As I write, I can picture you in Heaven with your Kittydear, wearing native garb, sitting with bare feet, cross-legged India style, around a campfire with boys and girls who would be laughing and singing *John Jacob Jingleheimer Schmidt*.

I see you challenging those same kids to learn how to put the puzzle ring together and then explaining the meaning of the square written near the message from St. Luke 2:52.

I visualize you in the pulpit explaining to your Boy Scouts your own simple personal rules for happiness.

>Free your heart from hatred - Forgive.
>
>Free your mind from worries. Most never happen.
>
>Live simply and appreciate what you have.
>
>Give more.
>
>Help others.
>
>Expect less.

I know you believed in world peace and international understanding. You knew Gandi and Nehru and were a supporter of India's independence. You cherished the peaceful ways of non-violence practiced by

Gandi and his followers. You also believed in the manly attributes of George Washington, surviving in the wilderness, cooking over outdoor fires, playing physical games, taking Boy Scouts on hikes into Kashmir. I can see that you and Kitty still love India and the Indian people – humans who have lived a ten thousand year epic that survives today.

I also know that you quietly and humbly left us without attaining your goal of being the oldest graduate to march in the Princeton parade. Your son John's eulogy spoke of your life's work. He told all who knew you that what you did was not insignificant and that you were as close to being Christ-like as any of us on Earth can be.

It's been almost 70 years since I met you and my own clock is ticking. Years have gone by very fast, but I still hear your message. For me, and thousands of others, knowing you showed us a way to life-long transformation – that it is a marathon, not a dash.

I was touched by you and wish that I could walk and talk with you again and maybe show you that your message worked for at least one troubled kid, me. Thanks to you my life has been good. You were a much-loved schoolteacher and administrator who connected with everyone on a human level.

In closing, my life-long mentor, "Vijaiji," as you were aptly named by your Indian friends, I know now what you would ask us all if you were standing here, "Are you ready

to live the four-square □ way and take up a life's work, to do good? If so, Live it!"
　　Your Secret Pal,
　　Lamba Singh □

PS: You will always be in my heart.

Appendix A
Bibliography

Personal Letters, M. Martin Lall, India, 2009.
"Progressive Revelation," Personal E-mail, Pastor Bill Simpson, November 13, 1999.
Wild at Heart: Discovering the Secret of a Man's Soul, John Eldredge, Thomas Nelson, 2001.
Wild at Heart: Field Manual, John Eldredge, Thomas Nelson, 2002..
Why It's Important to Know about India, Ainslie T. Embree, A History Institute Presentation, 2006.
A Whole Life's Work: Living Passionately, Growing Spiritually, Lewis Richmond, Atria Books, 2005.
What is Your Life's Work? Bill Jensen, Harper Business, 2005.
The Purpose Driven Life: What on Earth am I here for? Rick Warren, Zondervan, 2002.
Goodbye Mr. Chips!, originally published 1934, James Hilton, Little Brown Books for Young readers, , 2004.
To Serve Them All My Days, R. F. Delderfield, Source Books, 1972.
Amazing Grace, Mary Hoffman, Dial, 1991.
Facing the Giants, Max Lucado, Thomas Nelson, 2006.
Tuesdays with Morri, Mitch Album, Doubleday, 1997.
The Way Back to Mayberry: Lessons of a Simple Time, Joey Fann, H&B Publishing, 2001.
Chicken Soup for the Soul, Jack Canfield and Mark Victor Hansen.
Papers of Reverend Henri Rabb Ferger, Division of Rare & Manuscript Collections, Carl A. Kroch Library, Cornell University.
Conversations with Martha Ferger, widow of John Ferger, Henri's son, 2004-2009.

Wanless of India: Lancet of the Lord, Lillian Emery Havens Wanless, W.A. Wilde, 1944.
The Last Human Freedom, Alexander Green, Spititual Wealth, Friday, February 15, 2008.
The Birth of Twin Nations, Taylor, Carl E., M.D., F.R.C.P. (C.), December 18, 1947, Memorial Hospital, Fatehgarh, India.
www.Boyslife.org.
www.Scouting.org.
Author's Interview about Life in India, Dr. Krishna Meenakshi Moorthy, Ph.D., January 28, 2009.
Christ of the Indian Road, E. Stanley Jones, The Abington Press, 1925.
The Fading of an Era: The Last Missionaries in the Punjab, Mark Juergensmeyer, Ph.D., Alliance for Excellent Education.

Dr. Juergensmeyer is associate professor of ethics and the phenomenology of religions at the Graduate Theological Union, Berkeley. His article appeared in the *Christian Century*, December 22, 1976, 1144-1149. Copyright by The Christian Century Foundation; Avenue, NW, Suite 901, Washington, DC 200036, Phone 202-828-0828, www.all4ed.org, updated February 2009. Current articles and subscription information can be found at www.christiancentury.org. Used by permission.

Appendix B
The Boy Jesus at the Temple
(From BibleGateway.com)

    Every year His parents went to Jerusalem for the Feast of the Passover. When He was twelve years old, they went up to the Feast, according to the custom. After the Feast was over, while his parents were returning home, the boy Jesus stayed behind in Jerusalem, but they were unaware of it. Thinking he was in their company, they traveled on for a day. Then they began looking for him among their relatives and friends. When they did not find him, they went back to Jerusalem to look for him. After three days they found him in the temple courts, sitting among the teachers, listening to them and asking them questions. Everyone who heard him was amazed at his understanding and his answers. When his parents saw him, they were astonished. His mother said to him, "Son, why have you treated us like this? Your father and I have been anxiously searching for you."

    "Why were you searching for me?" he asked. "Didn't you know I had to be in my Father's house?" But they did not understand what he was saying to them.

    Then he went down to Nazareth with them and was obedient to them. But his mother treasured all these things in her heart. And Jesus grew in wisdom and stature, and in favor with God and men.

Appendix C
Understanding India's Culture

India has a population of over 1 billion people and is the world's largest democracy. With a labor force of about 500 million, 60 percent is employed in agriculture or agriculture-related industries that contribute only about 22 percent of the GDP.

India is also a country driven by its religious beliefs, dominated by Hindus (83 percent), followed by Muslims (only 11 percent of India's population but the world's third-largest Muslim population of about 115 million), Sikhs (2 percent), and Christians (2 percent). Hindi is the language spoken by 30 percent of the population, but its people speak 24 other languages. English is one of the 14 official languages. India's economy has been a mixture of traditional village farming, modern agriculture, and handicrafts, but an economic revolution has brought a myriad of modern industries and support services.

Starting in 1991, India has gradually opened up its markets through economic reforms by reducing government controls on foreign trade and investment. Privatization of public-owned industries and of some sectors to private and foreign players has continued amid political debate.

Recent government reforms have thrown open the economy and begun a liberalization to reduce controls on production, trade, and investment. The country's arms (outreach) are extended to foreign investment particularly infrastructure sectors. India has a growing number of international airports, and the railway system is the largest in Asia and the fourth largest in the world. An excellent national highway system connects all major cities, maritime ports and the export-processing zones at Kandia, Mumbai (Bombay), Calcutta, Falta, Cochin, New Okha, and

Visakhapatnam. Measured by purchasing power parity (PPP), the economy of India is the fourth largest in the world and it is the second fastest growing major economy in the world. The GDP growth rate, as of the first quarter of 2006, is 9.1 percent.

India's large English-speaking middle class has contributed to the country's growth. Outsourcing has become a major base of tech companies for future targeted research and development, including the likes of Google, IBM, and Microsoft. All this has helped the services sector to increase its share of the economy to approximately 50 percent. India is also a major exporter of financial, research, and technology services.

Appendix D
India in Henri's Time

As long as 9000 years ago, India's first-known permanent settlements developed into the famous Indus Valley culture. Here the Punjab trade routes brought vast empires together, contributing to world progress and wealth. India's civilization provided art, literature, history, and religion long before the British stepped upon Hindu soil.

Why were the British there in the first place?

Following the success of Portugal and Spain's colonization in South America and Africa, British's dominion over the Indian subcontinent began. In December 1600, Queen Elizabeth I granted a royal charter to the British East India Company to begin trade with India. By 1608 the first ships arrived, and in 1617 the Mullah Empire granted trading rights to the "Company."

Before the end of the first decade of the 18th century, the Company became a nation of its own on the Indian subcontinent. The Viceroy of India administered the princely states as well as present-day India, Pakistan, and Bangladesh.

The people of India were never content with British rule and rightly so. Equal job opportunities were not allowed. British people with high positions in government service or officers in the army were advanced automatically.

In 1885 lawyers and professionals from all parts of India and representing various religions formed the Indian National Congress. Members debated political and economic reforms and the future of India, searching for ways Indians could achieve equal status with the British.

Soon Muslims made it known that they thought the National Congress was a Hindu organization aiming for eventual Hindu rule. In 1906 several Muslim leaders, encouraged by the British, formed the All-India Muslim League, seeking to give Muslims a voice in political affairs.

When the British divided the state of Bengal into separate Hindu and Muslim sections, Indians protested with a boycott of British goods and a series of bombings and shootings. In an effort to stop the violence, the British introduced reforms that enlarged the viceroy's executive council to include an Indian and also allowed Indians to elect representatives to the provincial legislative councils.

American presence, mostly church groups who built excellent schools, hospitals, and colleges, was already growing. Yankee clipper ships began visiting British India in the nineteenth century.

In the midst of these significant changes, Henri Ferger arrived, according to his diary, precisely at, "5:49 September 30th, 1910, in Rawalpindi, just 32 days, lacking 10 minutes after leaving home."

When World War I broke out in 1914, Henri was in the States studying for his masters and divinity degrees. By the time he and Kitty returned to India in 1915, Britain had already declared that India was also at war with Germany. In return for Indian troops fighting in many parts of the world, the British promised more reforms and agreed to let Indians have a greater role in political affairs. During that war India faced two problems, supplying Britain with fighting soldiers at the same time they were maneuvering for their independence from Britain.

In March 1919 the British passed laws that tried to control protests by attempting to restrict political liberties and rights, including the right to trial by jury. Demonstrations against the government increased such that on April 13, 1919, thousands of Indians assembled in an enclosed area in Amritsar City in the Sikh state of Punjab. Troops entered the meeting place, blocking the entrance. The British commander ordered the soldiers to open fire on the unarmed crowd, killing about 400 people and wounding about 1,200.

The Amritsar Massacre proved to be a turning point. From then on, Indians demanded complete independence from British rule.

By 1920 Mohandas K. Gandhi, a leader in the Indian independence movement, persuaded the National Congress to adopt his program of nonviolent disobedience. His program included boycotting British goods, refusal to pay taxes, and to stop using British schools, courts, and government services. Some Indians gave up well-paying jobs that required them to cooperate with the British. Gandhi changed the Indian National Congress from a small party of educated men to a mass party with millions of followers.

Gandhi in 1930 led hundreds of followers on a 240-mile protest march against the Salt Acts that made it a crime to possess salt not bought from the government. At the sea they made salt from seawater. That march as well as other acts of civil disobedience forced the British to give the Indian people more political power. In 1931 Gandhi and the Viceroy, Lord Irwin, signed an agreement in which Gandhi agreed to give up his campaign of civil disobedience, and the British agreed to release thousands of political prisoners.

Meanwhile, the Muslim League had become more politically active. In 1934 Mohammad Ali Jinnah, an important Congress leader, was chosen to head the Muslim League. Under Jinnah's leadership, the league won a number of seats in the provincial legislatures, and party membership increased rapidly. The provincial elections of 1937, however, showed that most Muslims still supported the Indian National Congress.

Jinnah increased his political activity and declared that the Congress could not speak for Muslims. In 1940 he demanded that a new country be carved out of India for Muslims. The name Pakistan, *"land of the pure"* in Urdu, was chosen for this proposed nation. According to Jinnah, India was to be for Hindus and Pakistan for Muslims.

The Indians continued to demand independence. Britain kept promising independence after the war, but members of the Indian National Congress demanded immediate self-government instead, and they refused to support the war effort.

In 1942 Henri Ferger received the Kaiser-i-Hind Silver Medal from the British government for public service contributions during World War II as a member of the St. John Ambulance Association. At that time Henri was principal and manager of the Farrukhabad Christian High School in Fatehgarh. He could not become involved with the politics of WWII except as it concerned India's participation. Very interested in supporting Indian independence, he had to be careful; the American Presbyterian mission could not seem to be opposing the British government.

At the conclusion of the war in 1945, Congress leaders were released, and negotiations for independence were resumed. The British declared early in 1946 that they would grant India independence if Indian political leaders could agree among themselves on a form of government. Britain sent a special cabinet mission to India, but the Congress and the Muslim League could not settle their differences.

To show its strength and to warn the British not to make a separate agreement with the Congress, the Muslim League declared August 16, 1946, as Direct Action Day. On that day, Muslims held nationwide demonstrations calling for the establishment of Pakistan. Bloody rioting broke out between Muslims and Hindus in Calcutta (now Kolkata); similar violence later occurred elsewhere in India.

In 1947 Indian and British leaders agreed to partition (divide) the country into India and Pakistan. They saw no other way to end the violence.

India became an independent nation on August 15, 1947, Pakistan the day before. Partition was accompanied by more violence and bloodshed, and Gandhi fell victim to it. He was assassinated on January 30, 1948, while on his way to a prayer meeting in New Delhi.

Appendix E
Birth of Twin Nations

Dr. Carl E. Taylor, M.D., F.R.C.P. (C.), then director of Memorial Hospital, Fatehgarh, U. P. India, first expressed the term "Birth of Twin Nations" in his essay of the same title, published December 18, 1947. He used the analogy to show the uncertainty of the division of India into two parts.

No treatment of Henri and Kitty's time in India would be complete without explaining how their life was greatly affected during the India and Pakistan partitioning process. Missionaries first and educators second, they had to be careful of their activities. Yet they loved their boys and girls and felt strongly about the suffering during that treacherous period.

In that terrible year of 1947, Taylor wrote, "The birth pangs of liberty are cruelly painful. Among the women of the India, zenanasa, the long-standing deficiency disease of rickets, distorts the birth passages and causes many complicated deliveries, Caesarian operations, and stillbirths.

"Ancient India is giving birth to twin independent nations. Her long-standing deficiency diseases are making her delivery long and complicated. We are all hoping that the Caesarian section of civil war or the stillbirth of the coming again under outside rule will not be necessary. From present indications we can still hope that the final world verdict will be "mother and twins doing fine."

Independence from Britain didn't come until 1947 with partition of British India into India and Pakistan along religious lines. This was accompanied by horrific riots in both countries as Hindu and Muslims attacked each other, providing an enduring image of a region torn by religious strife. The beginning of the bitter estrangement between India and Pakistan was over Kashmir.

Pop watched in horror as his boys, Hindu and Moslem alike, were caught in the partitioning. As principal of a school, he had to stay neutral, but as a missionary he could help as he did for World War II as an ambulance driver.

With partition came more violence and bloodshed. As Hindus and Sikhs in Pakistan fled to India, and Muslims in India fled to Pakistan, more than 10 million people became refugees, About half a million people were killed in Hindu-Muslim riots.

One state that initially merged into neither India nor Pakistan was Kashmir where Pop Ferger and his family lived and worked. Pakistani Muslims launched an invasion to take Kashmir by force, and the war between India and Pakistan continued until 1949, when the United Nations (UN) arranged a cease-fire and set up a truce line.

As Doctor Taylor tells us, "The need for the spirit of love is brought into sharp focus by the intensity of the hatred between the two major communities. A question on everyone's lips is, 'Who started the riots?' Much adrenalin is being wasted all over India in verbal attempts to place blame on members of the opposite community.

"The killing was started by armed bands sometimes escorted by men in police or military uniform. They would break into shops and houses of the minority community. They would loot, kill, and abduct the women of a suitable age. The members of the minority community then gathered for self-protection in larger houses and compounds. In order to get them out, terrible devices were used...

"As the first wave of killing passed and government control again began to be felt, the staggering task of evacuation and the transfer of population started. Well over four million people were moved each way. I believe historically true that there have been few mass tragedies to equal this uprooting. Most of them went in foot convoys of 40,000 to 70,00 people and 3,000 to 4,000 carts, stretched along seven miles of road, traveling an average of ten miles a day for a total distance of 100 to 2000 miles or more, every step being haunted by terror of imminent fratricidal attack...

"The killing reached its climax in the refugee train attacks. The sheer bestiality and brutality of these attacks is incomprehensible to civilized mind, and yet they were performed by people who had been considered civilized. The refugee trains themselves were loaded with over 500 people per car with all their household effects. An average train carried between 4,000 and 5,000 people. They packed each compartment so tightly that suffocation was not uncommon. They covered the roof with top-heavy loads of luggage and held them on by sitting on them, and they glued themselves to every ledge and crevice on every surface of the train.

"The attackers were highly organized gangs known as "jathas," composed largely of refugees who had escaped from the other side with heavy losses in their own families.

"The trains were stopped by having someone planted to pull the emergency chain, or by obstructing the track. If the military guard offered resistance, they were attacked by some of the gang while the rest systematically went through the cars slaughtering and maiming...

"Many cases were hacked, stabbed, and slashed as many as twelve times in the most indescribable forms of mutilation. I have seen the casualties from several attacks and have had the unpleasant job of picking up wounded along the railway tracks for emergency surgery. It is a shaking thing. The worst incident about which I have heard was told by a Gurkha captain on duty in Amritsar when the Hindu station master arranged to have a Moslem refugee train stopped between two Sikh refugee trains. As a result Amritsar station was literally bathed in blood...

"Very soon after we started our work, the government asked us to take over a job which they admitted they were unable to handle. The large mass of Hindu-Sikh refugees were in Pakistan, with practically no medical care and vice versa with the Moslems...

"Finally things reached such a pitch of demoniac viciousness that God took a hand and the flood came. I would venture to say that there have been few floods since the time of Noah that have taken the toll of life that this one did. For three days in late September the whole of Punjab, arid especially the Himalayas north of Punjab, was inundated in a steady downpour. The flood that resulted covered the riot torn area as though trying to wash away the blood...

"The greatest loss of life was due to the fact that refugee foot columns had been seen moving along the roads when the rains hit them...

"Miles before we reached the area the stench greeted us in an almost palpable cloud. The penetrating sweetish-foul odor of rotting flesh seemed to take up permanent residence in our nostrils and I am sure I will still be smelling decaying carcasses months from now. This odor and the ubiquitous latrine odor are my most vivid memories of Punjab...

"Since no Hindu doctors could be sent to Pakistan, and since we enjoyed the confidence of all communities and could go without impunity wherever necessary, it was arranged that we should provide the medical care for those refugees in Pakistan. We worked as a mobile unit under the Military Evacuation Organization and moved from one troubled spot to another as necessary by outbreaks of epidemics. A buzzing canopy of flies covered the area. The death zone was about 10 to 15 miles in extent with bodies littered throughout. They were bloated, actively popping, or deflated after popping...

"The third catastrophe to hit Punjab and with a higher killing quotion than either communal fighting or floods, was disease. With this we found our job. A more ideal set-up for the spread of epidemics can scarcely be imagined that those malnourished, demoralized hordes exposed to the elements without any semblance of sanitary precautions. Nature seemed to be experimenting, to see just how much squalor and filth humans could survive in. The resistance of the people to these diseases is therefore high..."

Note that triage, the process of prioritizing sick or injured people for treatment according to the severity of the condition or injury, had to be used in these cases.

Taylor wrote, "The contribution that Indian Christians have made in these times is particularly noteworthy. They have brought a real message of reconciliation to their own brothers through their lives...

"Our biggest epidemic problem has been cholera. Small epidemics have been frequent and our unit has had to deal with three major ones...

"We have done scores of thousands of cholera inoculations...

"Next to cholera our greatest concern was smallpox and we did see two small epidemics which were largely self-limited. In some areas malaria was almost epidemic and we did extensive DDT spraying...

"India is finding her way through the vale of travail, blood, and sorrow towards liberty and will make a significant contribution to world peace and progress. For out of such testing character is built...

"I am sending a few shots taken by Henri Ferger who was able to join our unit to photograph our work, although not until much later."

It should be noted that the United States endeavored, without much success, to follow a neutrality policy. That attempt ended, however, in the 1950s, when the United States, in the search for Cold War allies, gave military support to Pakistan, thereby souring relations with India.

Although British India had become partitioned, an agreement also had to be reached with the princely states. Most local rulers agreed to merge their states into India. In return, the Indian government offered them annual payments. A few princely states joined Pakistan.

The war between India and Pakistan lasted until 1949, when the United Nations arranged a cease-fire and set up a truce line.

Appendix F
J. Fred Ferger Obituary

"Mr. J. Fred Ferger was born at Lawrenceburg, Indiana, July 20, 1861. His parents were Herman and Eliza (Wirth) Ferger, both German. He was educated in the schools of Lawrenceburg, and graduated in 1876. He married Miss Julia W. Rabb, Sept 20, 1887, and they moved to Chattanooga the same year, Mr. Ferger becoming bookkeeper in a bank. In 1888 he engaged in the real estate and insurance business with C G Fletcher, whose interest he purchased in 1890. Then Mr. Ferger associated himself in the same business with his brother, Herman Ferger, the firm name chosen being J Fred Ferger & Bro. In 1907 the firm name was changed to Ferger Bros, and from that date the firm has been one of the most extensive in real estate operations and insurance that ever did business in Chattanooga, having established the Ferger apartments, the Ferger building and Ferger Place, besides owning and controlling many other business and residential properties.

"Mr. Ferger was a Knight of Pythias, being a member of Keystone lodge. He was long a member of the chamber of commerce, and was at times a director in the organization. He was a very active and conspicuous church worker, and also a director in the local Young Men's Christian association.

"The children of Mr. and Mrs. Ferger are the Rev. Henri Rabb Ferger, Miss Nellie Ferger, Miss Margaret Ferger, and Wirth Ferger. The Rev. Henri Ferger has long been a missionary in India, and head of a boy's school supported by the mission. Miss Nellie went to India as a missionary in 1918."

http://www.tngenweb.org/hamilton/obits.htm

Appendix G
Founding the Boy Scouts

The founder of the Boy Scout movement, Robert Stephenson Smyth Baden-Powell, then a colonel and later a lieutenant general in the British army, returned to England a national hero for defending the town of Mafekeng (now Mafikeng) South Africa for seven months (217 days) October 1899 to May 1900 during the 2nd Boer War.

Several of Baden-Powell's military books, written for reconnaissance and scout training in his African years, were already widely read. Many boys and young men were avidly reading his book *Aids to Scouting,* a military training manual that taught soldiers techniques such as observation and tracking.

B-P, as he was affectionately called, met with various influential people in youth movements across the country and was persuaded to write a version of the book aimed at teenage boys. He tested his ideas during a camping trip on Brownsea Island that began in August 1907, the year Henri began at Princeton. B-P's experiment is now seen as the beginning of Scouting.

Based on the success of his earlier books and what he learned at Brownsea Island, B-P wrote a new version for youth readership. *Scouting for Boys* was initially published in 1908 and printed in six fortnightly parts that sold very quickly.

Originally intended as a supplement to the programs of youth organizations that were already in existence like the Boy's Brigade and Boy's Clubs, other youth movements bought the book. Soon B-P realized that some form of support organization was required.

The answer: Boy Scouts.

(Wikipedia)

Appendix H
Guide with Helps

Remember the key ideas:
The Pop Ferger story.
Indian puzzle ring
The four foundations: Mind, Body, Social Qualities, and Spirit.
St. Luke 2:52
Teaching in India
Founding Hindu Boy Scouts
The author's story.
How you think determines how you behave.

Discuss each of the following:
Mind
Challenge yourself
Onward, upward
More than the basics
Higher education
Orderly
Creative
Possibility thinker
Taking the opportunities
Testing yourself
Failure
Regroup, revisit
Focus
Determination
Attitude
Inter-people and intra-people
Abusive use of the mind
Positive use of the mind

Strategy/goals
Lifetime education

Body
Food
Sports
Testing yourself
Lifetime exercise
Sex
Use it or lose it
Not abusive
Temperance

Social Qualities
Be your own person -- not in the crowd, nor a crowd pleaser.
Concern for others
Other people oriented
Kind-hearted
Love
Community
Team work
Your own corporate culture -- write it yourself!
Look out for your people
Proud but not arrogant
Listen

Spirit
What do we mean?
It's inside your heart
Whose spirit?
Belief in a God? Something?
Based on what?
Does it make a difference?
    Bible: Old, New
    Koran

New Age
Beyond Saturday and Sunday
Get up. Get on your feet!!
Failure, rejection
Overcome!

The Four-Square Life
Traveling the long road
Was it worthwhile?
The full and rich life
Person of substance
Not about money
Your legacy
When it's over will you have touched as many as Pop touched?
What will your obit and headstone say?

Reaching Out
Be like Pop
Contribute
Participate
Take the message a step farther.

In today's world, I find it useful to ask these questions.
What changes are happening in your country?
Who am I?
How do you see yourself?
How do you fit in the changing times?
What can you do to make a difference in the world?
Are you a leader?
What is leadership?
How will you become a leader?
How do others see you?
Are you true to who you are?
What is your life's purpose and goals?
How do you plan to fulfill your potential?

In Conclusion

What are the stepping-stones to achieving your goal? If you want to rise, you must figure out the right 'stepping-stones' to take you to your target. Keep in mind that climbing stepping-stones is not easy – you must put in the time and work hard.